The Confiden

CW01023778

Even the best teachers are beset by doubts, assailed by excessive workload and struggle to juggle the job with their busy lives. *The Confident Teacher* offers a practical, step-by-step guide to developing the habits, characteristics and pedagogy that will enable you to do the best job possible.

This invaluable text unveils the tacit knowledge of great teachers and combines it with respected research and popular psychology. Covering topics such as organisation, using your body language effectively, combatting stress, managing student behaviour, questioning and feedback, and developing confident students, it shows how you can build the confidence and skill to flourish in the classroom.

Offering unique insights into the emotions experienced by teachers, this book will be an essential resource for all qualified and trainee teachers wanting to reach their full potential in this challenging but rewarding profession.

Alex Quigley is Director of Teaching and Learning at Huntington School, UK.

The Confident Teacher

Developing successful
habits of mind, body
and pedagogy

Alex Quigley

LONDON AND NEW YORK

First published 2016
by Routledge

2 Park Square, Milton Park, Abingdon, Oxon OX14 4RN
and by Routledge
711 Third Avenue, New York, NY 10017

Routledge is an imprint of the Taylor & Francis Group, an informa business

British Library Cataloguing in Publication Data
A catalogue record for this book is available from the British Library

Library of Congress Cataloging in Publication Data
Names: Quigley, Alex, author. Title: The confident teacher : Developing successful habits of mind, body and pedagogy / Alex Quigley.
Description: New York, NY : Routledge, 2016. | Includes bibliographical references.
Identifiers: LCCN 2015045915 | ISBN 9781138832336 (hardback) | ISBN 9781138832343 (pbk.) | ISBN 9781315627328 (ebook)
Subjects: LCSH: Teachers--Psychology. | Effective teaching. | Self-confidence.
Classification: LCC LB2840.Q54 2016 | DDC 371.102--dc23
LC record available at http://lccn.loc.gov/2015045915

ISBN: 978-1-138-83233-6 (hbk)
ISBN: 978-1-138-83234-3 (pbk)
ISBN: 978-1-315-62732-8 (ebk)

Typeset in Celeste and Optima
by Saxon Graphics Ltd, Derby
Printed in Great Britain by Ashford Colour Press Ltd.

Freya and Noah,
Waves
I dedicate this book to you both with all my love. I cannot wait to see you unleash yourselves with confidence upon this world.

Katy,
Thank you for ticking the good bits and fixing the flaws... in the book. Your unshakeable belief in me makes everything feel possible. Love, A.

Contents

Contents

Acknowledgements

There are many people whose ideas frequent much of this book and whose wisdom I attempt to distil: some are named and many are hidden. I am thankful to you all.

Most of my ideas have emerged from my work with people at Huntington School, York. I want to acknowledge them all, but I'd run out of ink. You know who you are: *thank you.*

Many people have kindly contributed to the book, so I would like to acknowledge the following for their words of wisdom and giving the time to furnish me with a quotation: Doug Lemov, Dr Lee Elliot Major, Andy Day, Jill Berry, John Tomsett, Harry Fletcher-Wood and Martin Robinson.

Thank you to Katy Gilbert (my better half) and Helen Day for your excellent feedback. To Mark Healy and Marc Smith, thank you for bringing your psychology expertise and insightful feedback to bear during the drafting of the book.

1 Introduction

Every teacher needs to improve, not because they are not
good enough, but because they can be even better.

Dylan Wiliam

I arrived for my first day at school as a teacher on a crisp
September morning in York. The beautiful city was my
new home of little over a week. As I passed the threshold
of the school gates, the freshness of the air was startling.

I had visited the school for my interview, then once or
twice over the summer holiday in a mad scramble to
prepare myself for the harsh baptism of a new career. It
patently hadn't worked. I felt like my near frantic lack of
confidence was on show for all to see – writ large in my
every word and action.

My mind lay open to an array of fears and anxieties.
What if I screwed this up? What if the students simply
laughed me out of the classroom? Despite a year of training,
coupled with as much planning as I could muster over the
summer holiday, I still felt spectacularly unprepared.

In a desperate attempt to assert some control over my
rabid nerves, I had scripted each moment of each lesson of
my first day, all by hand, in painstaking detail. I had

arrived at school an hour early so I could prepare myself and becalm my nerves.

After weeks of waiting, with quiet dread, it was time to stand at the front of the class and teach. For the first time, no teacher or mentor was sitting there watching – both a liberating and a frightening truth. I fumbled with the board pen to write the title and date. Blowing shallow breaths, I attempted to remember my script, before shuffling back to the teacher desk to read it over.

The students gazed at me with something like curiosity and the cool indifference that only teenagers can cultivate with such ease.

I began.

The whole day seemed a desperate act of masking my raw fears. And yet, nothing terrible happened. No eureka moments were to be had. At the end of the day I slumped in my teacher chair. I felt like an imposter, carrying off a deceitful trick while no one was looking. That surreptitious feeling was intermingled with a near overwhelming tiredness.

Despite the exhaustion, a germ of confidence in myself, and what I believed I could do as a teacher, was sown.

I realised soon after that teaching was very much an act of confidence. I could learn to teach successfully with committed effort – sometimes painstakingly so – but learn nonetheless. It was effort, commitment and the support of my fellow teachers that developed my expertise, but it was confidence in myself, and my belief that I could make a difference to the lives of my students, that helped me persist in reaching that goal.

Challenging times

Margaret Mead once stated that we shouldn't underestimate the power of a few committed people to change the world.

I have always held by her optimism and, for me, teachers have already been at the vanguard of the committed few.

My confidence in the power of teaching comes from my lived experience and from the influence of working with so many brilliant professionals, but if you read the papers you may be forgiven for judging the teaching profession as in crisis.

Are we at a negative 'tipping point' for the profession, where workload becomes insurmountable and we are no longer able to recruit enough teachers?

In countries the world over, the recruitment and retention of teachers is floundering. Stories of mountainous workloads, political interference and widespread teacher stress have dissuaded too many would-be teachers to enter the profession. Stress, burnout and dropping out have become an accepted part of the narrative of being a classroom teacher.

The statistics are chastening. In countries like England and America, nearly half of teachers leave the profession in the first five years; in Australia, the rate is nearer 30 per cent,[1] alongside Canada.[2] This attrition rate is damagingly high. A large-scale MetLife study of US teachers in 2012[3] found that teachers were stressed each of the seven days of the week by the job. Stress and teacher burnout are real problems that we no doubt need to address.

Clearly, we have a problem when far too many new teachers fail to ever achieve the confident degree of expertise that would carry them through to a satisfying, lifelong teaching career. The potential crisis of confidence in the teaching profession needs to be urgently addressed.

In truth, we cannot afford to wait for gone-tomorrow politicians to make the difference in helping teachers get better and helping them stay, indeed thrive, in the classroom.

Introduction

As one notable politician, and famous US president, said very recently, 'we are the change we seek'. Collectively, we can better mitigate the problems that attend workload and increase our stress. We can speak with a united voice in defence of our great profession. Together, we can fend off the media mud-slinging and concentrate upon becoming better teachers.

Making a difference

Despite the problems that no doubt attend our profession, most teachers prove a hardy and resilient bunch. For those of us who stick with teaching, we are nourished by our special experiences in the classroom, which give us confidence that what we do matters and makes a positive difference to the world.

Teachers may suffer from an image problem in the media, but scratch beneath the surface and talk to people about their personal experience of their school teachers and a different story emerges. Tease out some of those stories and we find that our teachers prove to be at the very heart of who we are as adults. Seldom do you meet a person whose life was not changed in some way, however subtly, by a special teacher.

The memories we create for our students may often be formed in unintended moments, appearing outside of our deliberately crafted lesson plan, but wherever they appear, we must harness their power.

Being a confident teacher is not about being blind to the issues faced by our profession, nor the obstacles that inhibit our students (both within school and in their lives outside of school), but it is about possessing a belief that we have the power to help our students to overcome those obstacles.

It is with such a belief, that a great teacher can trump the many barriers placed before our students, which spurs me on to write this book. With such belief, commitment and no little support, we can develop the confidence and skill to flourish in the classroom. It is such a nourishing confidence that sustains us through failure and helps us to grow professionally, until we attain something like expertise.

My hope is that this book can turn the cloudy notion of 'the confident teacher' into something concrete, tangible and useful. You can have teachers who display some 'natural' talent, but the majority of us are going about fashioning our self-confidence by developing our competence. If we are committed, and supported with the requisite conditions to grow as professionals, then we can reach the heights of an expert teacher.

My confidence was not quickly won after my scripted opening day of teaching. It was often a gruelling trek through long days in the classroom – facing my fears and failures daily and refusing to give up. My growing competence was met with growing self-confidence. The process was often maddeningly slow and gradual, spanning years, but it was essential in creating a deep groove of competence and self-confidence.

It wasn't until my third, or even fourth year of teaching, that I felt truly confident in my ability to teach all-comers in the sense of simply managing the room effectively. And yet, despite this improved control, I would continue to flail and fail on any given day. Still, I had – and have – lots to learn about the best strategies of expert teachers, but my deep reservoir of experience helps to sustain me. It is this type of self-confidence, rooted in competence and experience, which can help sustain every teacher.

So what exactly do I mean by self-confidence?

The answer is to be found rooted in the word itself. The definition comes from the Latin *confidere* – 'to trust'. Authentic confidence for a teacher stems from the trust we secure from our students and our colleagues. It becomes a trust we hold deeply within ourselves and helps guide what we do. We gain that trust by going the hard yards – the ultimate show of professional competence.

I don't wish to unduly romanticize the life of a teacher as being all hugs and high fives. Gaining trust from our students, or indeed our colleagues, is no swift or easy task. No class has yet stood atop their tables and quoted Walt Whitman at me – in a chorus of 'O Captain! My Captain!' – in unfettered adoration. I have not yet transformed a 'Gangsta's Paradise' into an ivory tower of learning. Alas, that is the stuff of Hollywood dreams. Instead, real teachers live by small, often unremembered, and seemingly unremarkable, acts of kindness.

Truthfully, boredom, frustration and struggle can too often attend our daily business. Despite this, teachers who possess a strong sense of *why* they do what they do in their working lives can better bear the many obstacles and buffers along the way. Sometimes teaching can feel tougher than the chewing gum clinging grimly to the underside of classroom desks, but with greater self-confidence we can feel optimistic about taking on the unique challenge each day.

When teachers feel in control, supported by their school leaders, their resilience and self-confidence can bloom. They can better fight stress, resist burnout and stick with teaching for longer.[4] We must replicate these conditions in each classroom and in every school. Of course, as teachers, we don't have the power to change the education system wholesale, but we can do the next best thing: we can change ourselves, what happens in our classroom and even our school.

Political meddling, unhelpful bureaucracy and workload issues may prove a universal experience for too many teachers across the world, but the compelling act of teaching and learning goes on. Teachers can – and do – make a difference. It is that which gives us purpose.

Notes

1   Watt, H.M.G. and Richardson, P.P.W. (2007), 'Motivational factors influencing teaching as a career choice: Development and validation of the FIT-choice scale', *The Journal of Experimental Education*, 75 (3): 67–202.
2   Karsenti, T. and Collin, S. (2013), 'Why are new teachers leaving the profession? Results of a Canada-wide survey', *Education*, 3 (3): 141–149.
3   'The MetLife survey of the American teacher' (2012), [Online]. Available at: www.metlife.com/assets/cao/foundation/ MetLife-Teacher-Survey-2012.pdf (Accessed: 10 June 2015).
4   Klassen, R.M. and Chiu, M.M. (2011), 'The occupational commitment and intention to quit of practicing and pre-service teachers: Influence of self-efficacy, job stress, and teaching context', *Contemporary Educational Psychology*, 36: 114–129.

Section 1
The confident mind

2 How much confidence is enough?

There is no perfect teacher, nor the perfect degree of confidence: the classroom is much too complicated for that. We must then face up to the complexity of our varying degrees of confidence.

We know that our confidence can fluctuate on a daily basis. We can be confident in one aspect of our teaching, indeed our lives (yes – teachers manage to sometimes muster a life beyond work), but that can have little bearing on other aspects of what we do. Any given teacher could prove a subject expert, whilst having little or no confidence that they can manage the behaviour of their classes adequately.

Therefore we need to break down each aspect of our self-confidence and do an honest appraisal of where we stand as a teacher. Let's make a start. Rate yourself on the rough-and-ready confidence continuum below, based upon your judgement of self-confidence in the following ten broad areas:

1 Your capacity to manage student behaviour successfully
2 Your command of your subject(s) knowledge
3 Your ability to speak to groups of fellow teachers
4 Your knowledge and understanding of how children learn
5 Your knowledge and understanding of common misconceptions in learning
6 Your capacity to manage your workload
7 Your capacity to manage your physical health
8 Your capacity to balance your work with your home life
9 Your sense of control when teaching in the classroom
10 Your sense of control over your teaching career

Unconfident   **Very Confident**

If we ask ourselves these questions then the natural next step is to probe a little further. If we are middling on our continuum for question 1, for example, we should then ask: what specifically can I do to develop my behaviour management? Also, we can ask: what support do I need to develop my competence and confidence in this aspect of my professional practice?

Let's take question 2: our subject knowledge. We can ask: how can I develop my subject knowledge further? What support do I need? Do I have the time to do this successfully? If I am pushed, what singular aspect of my subject knowledge can I develop to enhance my competence and grow my confidence? Of course the questions above are all related. It may well be that by improving our subject knowledge, we free ourselves up mentally in the classroom, thereby allowing ourselves to then better manage the behaviour of our students.

Take some time to reflect upon the patterns that emerge in your answers. Many teachers feel wholly competent and confident when in the thick of teaching in the classroom, but factors outside of the classroom can assail them with worry. Others feel confident dealing with their students and their colleagues personally, but their lack of knowledge in what they are teaching can diminish their confidence in their ability to be a good teacher.

Let's be realistic, some teachers manage their workload by compromising their home life. Confidence in one aspect of our working life can impact upon another. As you consider the patterns that emerge in your answers, more questions should arise about how you can better take control of your professional life. Hopefully, many of these questions can be addressed in this book.

We should not assume that bursting full of confidence in any of these aspects of our professional life is wholly desirable. Ironically, with too much confidence we may stop committing ourselves to the planning and preparation that ensured our success in the first place. All too easily, we may falsely mistake our confidence for actual competence.

Why being unconfident may be a good thing

Let us be careful here to not depict confidence as some miracle cure. Great minds have recognised the perils that attend confidence. It was the philosopher, Bertrand Russell who famously said:

How much confidence is enough?

The fundamental cause of the trouble is that in the modern world the stupid are cocksure while the intelligent are full of doubt.[1]

One of the lessons that emerge from my personal experience with colleagues is that many of the best teachers are bursting with brilliance, but they can easily struggle with a seemingly shallow well of self-confidence. Like Bertrand Russell stated, they are full of doubts, about themselves and their ability to teach well. Their practice isn't a show-stopping burst of personality; instead, it is something subtler and nuanced, even unconfident in some cases.

Let me share with you a portrait of Jack.

The small details of being in her lesson resonated with me. There was no grand opening to beguile the students. Instead, she listened intently to students as she welcomed them into the room: their questions and problems were swiftly attended to with a smile and a kind word.

Established routines were executed almost imperceptibly. Books, paper, homework and pens were all arranged in a subtle sweep. Honed and near-hidden routines, no doubt established with effort, funnelled students quickly to the task at hand.

Then to the teaching: a quick exercise in analogy and metaphor was then initiated with precision and clarity. Objects from their pencil case were to be transformed into the characters of the novel they had been reading. Minds were kindled with interest, books were opened, and soon an immersion into the world of their novel began.

Their understanding was teased out with deft questions. Students were selected by name and questions were pitched at just the right degree to see them volley back their insights. Without gimmicks or any extraneous detail, Jack exhibited her expert skill.

Like a swan, she would bear herself with calm and equanimity, even in the face of the most trying stresses. Everything she approaches about her job as a teacher is done with commitment and rigour. No specification is left unturned. No student work hacked off with little effort is accepted. Students *want* to work for her.

Like most of the best teachers I have known, she would often go unnoticed in the crowd. You would not describe her as a confident type. There are no special performances under lights. Instead, she applies herself with a steady effort. She would likely wear the mantle of the introvert with quiet comfort and composure, but with a concurrent steely determination. Her confidence would not prove obvious.

What would be obvious is her industry. Jack's success comes not from overconfidence, but from a conscious competence that stems from thorough planning, day by day, week by week. The lesson I describe has no doubt been taught before, honed and improved. Jack's experience matters, but it is her conscious effort to improve that marks out her excellence, rather than some inflated sense of her own importance.

We herald self-confidence as the answer to all our ills but too often self-confidence derives from ignorance rather than knowledge. We mistake confidence for loud bluster. Give me a quiet, unassuming but determined teacher, willing to go the hard yards when no one is looking, every time. That is my idea of authentic confidence, not a gaudy show of arrogance.

There is a fine balance. It is the 'Goldilocks principle of confidence'. We need to avoid possessing too little confidence, as that can prove debilitating and self-defeating, but we can't have too much self-confidence either, as arrogance is too often a springboard to stupidity. We need just the right degree of authentic confidence.

How much confidence is enough?

I love an anecdote about Pablo Picasso, which captures such an authentic confidence, hard earned from years of toil and skill.

It describes when Picasso was outside drawing away and a brash young woman came along and was insistent that he draw her. Being in a good mood, he played along. When he was finished he asked her for a fee. She asked him how much. Picasso answered with a weighty sum beyond her means, but worthy of his greatness. The woman shrieked, complaining that he had only taken five minutes over the drawing. Picasso replied that it had taken him a lifetime to be able to complete that five-minute drawing.

Great teachers develop their authentic confidence like Picasso honed his art: steadily, with deliberate practice, perseverance and passion. It can last a lifetime, but it results in a deep and sustaining satisfaction of a job well done.

Recognition of this fact can prove liberating. We can throw off the debilitating shackles of perfectionism (such perfectionism, unattainable and fundamentally damaging, is inextricably linked to professional burnout).[2] We can embrace our failures and our bad days (okay – our bad weeks) and then we can get on with aiming for steady improvements, just like Jack.

The great modern actor, Mark Rylance, gives the simple and distilled advice to new and young actors that to be successful you need to believe *you are enough*. Those three words, both simple and incredibly complex, are equally as instructive for teachers everywhere.

You are enough. Don't seek out perfection. Don't aim to be better than your colleagues – just aim to be the best version of yourself. This will be enough and it will give you enough self-confidence to persevere and to flourish.

Low self-confidence and the introverted teacher

The question 'How much confidence is enough?' is a tricky one, but we know that too little confidence can prove damaging. Weakened by stresses and pummelled by daily failures, it is too easy to lose our confidence. When our confidence is too low our teaching can unravel. A vicious cycle can ensue.

When our lessons are turning sour – perhaps students are misbehaving and we are losing control – in an act of self-preservation, we can be inclined to hide the evidence. It need only take a boss that lacks understanding, or a climate tainted by fear, and we mask our troubles.

In an attempt to survive the day, we can drop our standards just a little. A student can utter something that we know to be unacceptable, but we simply don't have the energy to take on the issue. Small losses accumulate. Students begin to target our lessons and challenge our authority. Tired and worn down, our willpower wanes and we lose our resilience in the face of such strife. Inevitably, our confidence suffers and we can go quiet.

In our society, where self-absorbed and self-promoting celebrities raise arrogance to an art form, introversion and shyness can become pathologised as a desperate failing. In her brilliant book, *Quiet*, Susan Cain shows how our society heralds extroversion as a prerequisite for success, when we really should take care to celebrate the skills of the introvert.

Susan Cain cites a study that claims one in three Americans is actually an introvert. Of course, any such personality label is a simplification, but it is clear that traits associated with introversion are more common than we think. Cain explores the genetic inheritance that can underpin introversion, and she opened up a world of understanding for many teachers.

Andy Day, a teacher and leader of Geography in East Yorkshire, has taught for over thirty years. Reading *Quiet* opened up Andy's understanding of introversion: 'I'm not sure I would have termed myself an "introvert" before coming across Cain's book. I was aware I preferred dinner with friends to a party, and I wasn't good at giving immediate responses to a problem. Instead, I preferred time to think it through, and needed to withdraw to a quiet place at lunchtimes, instead of the staffroom, to reflect, regroup and plan for the afternoon lessons.'

Though Andy's recognised his introverted behaviour, he knew this was different from his sense of self-confidence: 'I didn't lack confidence – as a child I sang solos in the church choir, played parts in amateur dramatics and could "perform". It took me some time, as a young teacher, to work out the appropriate "performance" in school. I spent my first two or three years failing in my attempt to adopt the roles I saw so effectively portrayed by others, all to disappointing effect.'

It was from this catalogue of apparent 'failures' that Andy realised he had to inhabit his own performance – one that was genuine and comfortably shouldered. Planning and preparation gave Andy confidence and experience helped him to solidify that confidence.

Such introversion, a common trait among teachers, is often wrongly conflated with shyness. Shyness can be defined as a feeling of apprehension or awkwardness in social situations and it can prove emotionally crippling at its extremes. Introversion, on the other hand, is not necessarily focused upon social anxiety, but instead it reflects a preference for solitude and reflection.

Many introverted teachers can exist happily in the social hubbub of a school, before withdrawing intermittently to reflect and recharge, just like Andy. Like most matters of our psychology, there is a complex continuum reflected in each of us. Perhaps you are a classic introvert, or an extrovert who thrives in large social groups, or maybe you exist somewhere in the middle – an *ambivert*. Ambiverts can get on comfortably in the midst of a crowd, but they distinctly relish some time alone.

Make a judgement about where you consider yourself to be positioned on the introvert/extrovert continuum:

Introvert	Extrovert
Being with people can prove draining	Being with people proves energising
You prefer to listen when in conversation	You prefer to initiate and lead conversation
You prefer to internalise your thoughts	You prefer to externalise your thoughts
You prefer to work individually	You prefer to collaborate with others
You prefer to work in a quiet classroom	You prefer to work in a busy classroom

Teaching is often considered an extrovert profession. We stand in front of large groups of students each day and we are forced to communicate with a sheer mass of people, forming many complex relationships, all day long. Surely then, extroversion comes naturally to teachers?

As Susan Cain relates, people easily equate a talkative disposition with intelligence, likeability and even competence. As role models for our students, many introverts amongst them, we should be mindful of exposing this stereotype.

We should ask: do we confuse an extrovert performance with great teaching? Do we misattribute confidence as extroversion?

How much confidence is enough?

Akin to self-confidence, our personality traits can be bound to our task at hand. Put a teacher in front of a class of youngsters and they can take a confident lead, practised in control and clarity. The self-same teacher, in a room full of teaching colleagues, may shrink back in mute stillness, or feel drained by the fears induced by such an experience (of course, plenty of extroverts suffer such fears in front of their peers too – as a performance can sometimes be separated from our personality).

We should herald the strengths of the teacher more naturally inclined toward introversion. Such a temperament can make for better listening skills. Rather than excitedly waiting to be heard, many people with more introverted personalities listen with acute intent. I have been struck many times in faculty meetings by such colleagues, who, quietly absorbing and synthesising information, would strike at the heart of the problem with a perceptive answer.

We should seek out such quiet decisiveness. Think of those colleagues you would describe as possessing quiet confidence and let us celebrate those colleagues. It may well accurately describe you!

Many of the wisest school leaders I have known have actually been quiet, humble and understated. Despite the correlation between leadership and extroversion, the capacity to speak after thinking deeply, characteristic of more introverted school leaders, can often be at the root of great leadership.

We should be careful of recognising our personality differences in the staffroom and the classroom. With better recognition of our personal differences, we can better grow our collective confidence and work together to utilise our best strengths.

We can ask ourselves more questions:

- Where do we stand on the introvert/extrovert continuum?
- How can we best seek out and utilise the personality strengths of our peers?
- Where do our students stand? How can we best nurture their development with this in mind?
- How can we create the conditions in our classroom, and our school, for us all to thrive with confidence?

Why too much self-confidence is a bad thing

When asking how much confidence is enough we must be clear that possessing too much self-confidence can prove unhealthy. By heralding the power of confidence, I need to sound a warning about the dangers of overconfidence. In an interview for *C-Span*, the writer, Malcolm Galdwell, put it best:

> *Incompetence irritates me, but overconfidence scares me. Incompetent people rarely have the opportunities to make mistakes that greatly affect things. But overconfident leaders and experts have the dangerous ability to create disaster.*[3]

An irony that attends all professions is that the most ignorant of people are more likely to believe that they are brilliant, whilst the most intelligent of people are just as likely to underestimate their abilities and be assailed by doubts. As Gladwell warns of the overconfident leader, we should also be wary of the overconfident teacher. Or worse still, we should worry about the overconfident school leader.

The world of self-help books and professional literature is indeed focused in on a lack of self-confidence and self-esteem, but it can be the overestimating of our abilities that can prove most damaging. It can manifest itself as teachers who won't listen, or be willing to learn, or school leaders who drive through wrong-headed changes that lead teachers to the brink of burnout and more.

I am with Malcolm – overconfidence scares me.

Of course, these words and fears are aimed at somebody else, right? You, *dear reader*, are not overconfident. You don't overestimate your abilities. You have unerring accuracy in your judgements of self. Indeed, you are a paragon of humility.

Wrong.

One of our very human traits is that we are in possession of a legion of mental biases that attend our every thought and action. If we didn't think we were better than average then we would likely struggle to get out of bed in the morning because of our crippling lack of confidence and our indecision. It is simple biology that drives us to erect our egos as towers of wisdom and understanding. And yet, recognising our predilection for overconfidence is a good way of keeping it in check.

Beating off the biases that fill us with too much confidence

I could present an array of evidence and studies that prove we all think that we are above average. Whether it is our looks, intelligence, likeability, listening skills, our ability to drive, or our professional skill; we think we are better than most. I'm no mathematician, but us all proving above average is pretty much a statistical impossibility. Still, we each possess the handy skill of blotting out such incriminating evidence.

This human trait is so pervasive that it has been enshrined in psychology as the 'Dunning- Kruger effect' – or put more simply, the 'Dumb and Dumber effect'. David Dunning, who originated the term, wrote an article with perhaps my favourite ever headline: 'We are all confident fools'.[4] Dunning relates the common sense notion that overconfidence stems from ignorance, but that very lack of expertise and self-awareness means that it goes unnoticed. In short, people don't know what they don't know: we possess unconscious incompetence.

It isn't just uneducated fools that are subject to this mental proclivity for overconfidence. Those of us who are highly educated prove little better, as we can think we know it all. In his research, Dunning showed that when people are faced with scientific-sounding terms that don't even exist, like 'meta-toxins' or 'bio-sexual', that people are prone to over-claim their knowledge of these terms and unwittingly expose their overconfidence.[5]

The evidence reveals that we should all guard against overconfidence and be humble about the boundaries of our knowledge.

We are fundamentally a protectionist species from a psychological standpoint. We create an armoury of mental shortcuts and we defend our decisions to the hilt, right or wrong. With this in mind, here are just a few of the shortcuts that bias our thinking and can lead to overconfidence:

- **Confirmation bias.** We like being right. So much so, we surround ourselves with people who think similarly to ourselves. Rather than being challenged, we receive confirmation of what we think and believe.
- **The availability heuristic.** As we are time-poor, we often seize at the best evidence available: what is directly in front of us. By doing so we can hamper a more sustained and deeper evaluation of our practice.
- **The sunk cost fallacy.** No one wants to fail (more on failure later in the book). If we have invested our time and energy in something at work, we are unwilling to let it go, or to stop doing it. This can lead to our flogging the proverbial dead horse.

- **Hindsight bias.** You knew this one was coming didn't you? We have an inbuilt inclination to confirm that we are always right. As such, we reconstruct events and our memory can distort reality to protect our delicate sense of self.
- **Illusion of transparency.** This particular flaw in our thinking reflects our tendency to overestimate the degree to which what we are thinking is known to others. We can explain a concept to our students but then be dumbfounded when they don't grasp the subtleties of our thinking. We should avoid such overconfident assumptions.
- **The backfire effect.** This is when people react to having their beliefs or views challenged by actually strengthening those self-same views. This reaction is responsible for a great deal of woe in the world and in the staffroom, but it is important for teachers to be open-minded about their practice and even their beliefs about education.
- **The mere exposure effect.** We like what we know and we know what we like. Our very familiarity with a teaching strategy, or a way of working, can lead us to stick with it through thick and thin, simply through the power of familiarity.

One way to inoculate ignorance is a shot of knowledge. We all need to recognise we are simply not that smart. By better understanding the flaws in our thinking, we can better ward off overconfidence and cultivate competence, with just the right degree of authentic confidence.

So how do we puncture our inflated self-image? How do we find just the right degree of authentic confidence?

Knowing our psychological cheat sheet of cognitive biases is a start, but we need to go further. One strategy is to consciously seek out constructive challenges to our thinking. This could be in the form of surrounding ourselves with critical friends and trusted colleagues.

Abraham Lincoln famously initiated his fabled 'team of rivals'. This group of politicians would robustly challenge each policy decision that was made. We can similarly ensure that our self-delusions and our capacity to 'group think' does not always win out, so that we can receive the benefits of being challenged.

We can actively seek out a constructive climate that challenges our thinking, without crippling our self-confidence. Following these instructions would be a positive start:

- Surround ourselves with critical friends. These need not necessarily be our official leaders – having honest, reflective conversations with our trusted colleagues can often prove most fruitful.
- Read evidence from as many sources as we can find to ensure our decisions are not simply a manifestation of our natural biases. Recognise that we will still pick our experts based on our favoured beliefs, which likely confirm how we currently teach and work. We teachers are a stubborn bunch!
- Be open to social networks that don't simply echo our views, but who instead challenge our beliefs and opinions in a constructive fashion.
- Treat failure as normal. By normalising failure, we can weaken the innate sense of threat that makes us rely so heavily on our mental biases for protection.

His confidence and her humility

How much confidence we possess can be bound to who we are, where we are from, and even whether we were born male or female.

How much confidence is enough?

The loud, extrovert male and the humble female: are they merely stereotypes or something more like reality? Like most things, the differences between individual male teachers and between female teachers will be more pronounced than a simple gender divide. Still, the classrooms and boardrooms of the world overtly favour men. This, in turn, fosters masculine overconfidence that can threaten to give confidence a bad name.

We know that it is not just social expectations and stereotyping of professional women that can have a damaging effect on female teachers' confidence. In her book, *Lean In*, a clarion call for women to seize their power at work, Sheryl Sandberg, Chief Operating Officer at the social media behemoth Facebook, appeals for women to conquer their instinctive *imposter syndrome* (the belief that we will be found out – that we are not good enough compared to others), to challenge societal expectations – taking a lead, proving ambitious, and possessing an authentic confidence in their work.

Jill Berry, a school leader in six schools over a span of thirty years, has commonly noted that women are more prone to *imposter syndrome* in comparison to men: 'I have worked with some excellent women teachers and leaders, but many have needed convincing of their own potential (it requires showing them what they're capable of, rather than simply telling them).'

Despite women outnumbering men in the teaching workforce, male school leaders still predominate. Again, authentic confidence matters.

Jill observed that too many female teachers only go for promotion 'after considerable persuasion' and that 'many women seem to be deterred from attempting something they don't believe they can do perfectly from the outset.' Humility is a great personal quality to have, but it should not hamper women from believing in their skill and will as a teacher, speaking up in meetings, challenging bad practice, or celebrating their successes.

The right amount of confidence, balanced against self-doubt, is required. Jill recognises the delicate balance: 'A degree of humility and self-doubt can actually make us *better* leaders – more considered, reflective leaders. Of course, too much self-doubt can be debilitating – it can render us incapable of making decisions and we can lose credibility among those we lead.'

There is no doubt that we can identify a mass of negative stereotypes about female professionals, including teachers, with depressing ease. In a Harvard study involving 20,000 eleven- to eighteen-year-old boys and girls, 'Leaning Out: Teen Girls and Leadership Biases',[6] both girls and boys favoured women in leadership roles, but only in traditional caring roles, whereas other professions, like politics, was seen as a male-only domain.

Negative messages about females taking a lead (of course, teaching is an act of leadership) become internalised early by females and males alike. Sheryl Sandberg encourages women to focus upon facing the internal obstacles first. These self-made obstacles, seeing ourselves as inferior to others, are under our control, and tackling them – both individually and in our classroom – is the first step to challenging the wider social issue of implicit and explicit sexism. By better understanding confidence, we can arm ourselves with the tools to break down barriers in our profession, whether it is barriers specifically related to women, or people with more introverted personality types.

For many women, a lived reality of being a teacher is balancing having children with being in the classroom. This can bring with it some very real obstacles. We know that there can be a 'baby penalty' paid by mothers that can be twofold. First, it puts a stopper, both implicit and explicit, on opportunities for women to take on leadership roles in school. Second, the extended absence of maternity leave can prove a disorientating and disempowering experience.

My own partner expressed how difficult maternity leave proved for her: 'I found going back to work after my maternity leave incredibly difficult. Not only did I feel like I'd lost a limb leaving my children, but returning to the work arena felt very alien after so long away. My confidence was at an all time low.'

She went on to describe how the changes had robbed her of her former competence: 'I found that I'd forgotten things that used to be second nature: some routines had changed, others I'd forgotten. Staff had changed, so all the hard work that I'd put into establishing myself as a hard-working, reliable member of staff before I left to have my baby, somehow felt obsolete on my return.'

Being robbed of confidence due to extended leave from work is not uncommon. When it is wedded with other societal barriers, we see the number of women becoming school leaders funnel in number. Too often female teachers experience a lifetime of subtle, or often less-than-subtle, attacks on their sense of self-confidence. If a man displays leadership qualities, an equivalent woman could easily be described as 'bossy'; if a man forcefully asserted their opinion in a meeting, a woman could easily be decried for being unladylike.

Happily, many female teachers and school leaders aren't waiting around for the slow burn of gradual change, whether they are deemed 'bossy' or not. In developing movements, like #WomenEd, we find teachers looking to break down the pervasive stereotypes that can inhibit women from taking up leadership positions in our schools and beyond. With such collaborative movements we can find a collective confidence that can only enrich our great profession.

Let us remember that the most intelligent teachers, female or male, may be full of doubts. They need authentic confidence to carry them forward to act. We know that some teachers display an unfounded arrogance that some label confidence, but if we go too far the other way, and we are too inhibited by doubt, then we will lack the psychological reserves to teach and lead with assurance.

IN SHORT...

- Too much confidence, like most things in excess, is no good thing.
- We should not confuse quiet introversion with being unconfident, nor should we mistake extroversion for excellence.
- A good defining quality of the teacher expert would be that they know the limits of their expertise and that this regulates their degree of self-confidence.
- Each of us, no matter how grounded or humble, is laden with our own mental biases. These can lead us to be overconfident in our practice and stop us seeking out the challenges that can positively change us and lead to self-improvement.
- To fend off overconfidence, we should seek out critical friends and we should challenge our intuitions with different sources of available evidence.
- Most of us experience 'imposter syndrome': the belief that we will be found out and not prove good enough. Such thinking may prick overconfidence, but we should be wary of such thinking paralysing us and thereby stultifying our personal development.
- Authentic confidence achieves a fine balance of humility, experience, self-belief and a keen sense of one's own weaknesses and strengths.

Notes

1   Russell, B. (1933), *Mortals and Others*, Essay title: 'The triumph of stupidity'. Essay date: 10 May 1933, page 203–204. Published by Taylor & Francis e-library.

2   Society for Personality and Social Psychology (2015), 'Perfectionism linked to burnout at work, school and sports', *ScienceDaily*. [Online]. Available at: www.sciencedaily.com/ releases/2015/07/150731105248.htm (Accessed: 2 August 2015).

3   Gladwell, M. (2009), 'C-Span interview – Q&A with Malcolm Gladwell', 30 November 2009. [Online]. Available at: www.c-span.org/video/?290341-1/qa-malcolm-gladwell (Accessed: 10 December 2014).

4   Dunning, D. (2014), 'We are all confident idiots'. Pacific Standard. 27 October 2014. [Online]. Available at: www.psmag.com/health-and-behavior/confident-idiots-92793 (Accessed: 10 January 2015).

5   Atir, S., Rosenzweig, E. and Dunning, D. (2015), 'When knowledge knows no bounds: Self-perceived expertise predicts claims of impossible knowledge', *Psychological Science,* 26: 1295–1303, first published 14 July 2015.

6   Richard Weissbourd and The Making Caring Common Team, 'Leaning out: Teen girls and leadership biases', Harvard Graduate School of Education. [Online]. Available at: http://sites.gse.harvard.edu/sites/default/files/making-caring-common/files/mcc_leaning_out_for_web.pdf (Accessed: 6 August 2015).

3 Developing self-confidence

It makes for a picture-perfect American dream.

Albert was born in 1925, the youngest of six siblings – all sisters. His Polish father and Ukrainian mother were both immigrants and homestead pioneers in the tiny town of Mundare, in Alberta, Canada (some fifty miles east of Edmonton). His father laid railroad track and both parents endured a harsh struggle to carve out their new lives for their young family from rocky ground.

Albert's school life was spent in a small, ramshackle building that housed all the students of the town, taught by only two (no doubt very strained) teachers. The entire high school mathematics curriculum simply comprised of a tattered textbook. Undeterred, Albert and his friends would emerge from their humble schooling with distinction, many going onto university, including Albert, with great success.

Albert would cite the courageous self-reliance of his parents as influential role models for his future life and his thinking. Both his parents helped build their town from nothing, alongside their young family. His father, no doubt still exhausted by grinding physical labour, would teach himself three languages. Albert would go on to learn much of his high school curriculum through a correspondence course.

A potent mix of intellect, resilience and determination would characterise Albert's early life.

Decades later, Albert Bandura would become one of the most celebrated and regularly cited psychologists in his field – behind only the likes of Skinner, Piaget and Freud. Such gritty self-determination and success is the stuff of Hollywood stories. The hero rising from humble beginnings, finding fame and renown, is the story that helped build modern Canada and North America alike.

His life story is a testament not only to a hardy heritage, but also how an unstinting belief in education, with a nourishing self-confidence and work ethic, can help us overleap the most difficult of circumstances.

I write about Albert Bandura, not primarily because he taught for years at Stanford University in California, or because he is a role model in showing us all how we can steer the direction of our professional lives, but because his theories provide us with a useable template for the confident teacher.

Albert spent much of his professional life defining his theory of *self-efficacy*. It is this theory that is instructive for teachers of all ages and stages.

The power of self-efficacy

The idea of self-confidence can too often prove a broad, loose and downright misused notion. Sugar-coated self-help gurus tout the power of confidence like it is some wonder drug to cure all of our ills. It isn't. It won't.

The Internet is littered with dreamy images of endless horizons and virgin beaches, scarred only with the optimism of confidence quotes emblazoned in delicate, italic fonts. Grains of truth about the powers of self-confidence are lost in the haze of bountiful beaches.

Albert's notion of self-efficacy offers us up a more precise tool. Something a teacher can grab a hold of and use to help develop their expertise in the classroom. To understand self-efficacy fully we need to untangle it from some other very similar terms:

- **Self-efficacy:** this is an individual's belief in their own ability to achieve a specific task, like teach their new science class successfully.
- **Self-concept:** this is an individual's perception of themselves, their identity and persona in a broader sense.
- **Self-esteem:** this is an individual's emotional evaluation of their own worth.
- **Locus of control:** this is similar to self-efficacy in that it is an individual's belief that their actions can make a difference.

Each of the above clearly affects each one of us, but I think that the remit of this book is to help teachers teach better – boosting our *self-efficacy* – and thereby developing our *locus of control.*

Essentially, the aim is to make clear how we can be a great teacher in practice and thereby believe we can make a tangible difference to the lives of our students. For me, this defines a confident teacher.

As this definition of teacher confidence is more concrete and more specific than self-esteem, it is much easier to develop. When I refer to teacher confidence from this point forward I want to sidestep the rather fuzzy notion of self-esteem, which is about a mass of complex emotions and beliefs, that proves much harder to develop than something concrete and distinct like managing the behaviour of a class of students.

There is a crucial point to delineate here: *self-esteem is simply feeling good about yourself, whereas self-confidence is feeling good about yourself because of what you can do.*

Self-confidence is specifically about how you feel about your abilities and it can vary from situation to situation, from task to task.

Take your students: they could have very high self-esteem, but they have no confidence in their ability to do mathematics. Similarly, a teacher can have shaky self-esteem that pervades their lives, including many of their personal and family relations, and yet they are undoubtedly an excellent teacher.

Of course, self-esteem is really important for our health and happiness, but it lies outside the remit of this book. It is a personality trait that can take decades to develop and change. Confidence isn't a personality trait, but is instead an expectation of success that fuels our motivation, and, crucially, it can be grown with practice.

Teacher confidence holds tremendous importance for us, especially given that it can be grown. Self-confidence in ourselves as a teacher can help deepen our motivation so that we persevere when we fail, or when times are tough. In essence, it is emotional and psychological fuel that helps drive us on, and through, to success.

Teacher confidence is also variable. It can ebb and flow through the course of a school day. This notion will sound familiar to every teacher. Given a morning class with your favourite group of hard-working students you may be high in confidence. After lunch, an older group of skulking teens may darken your classroom door. Given a troublesome prior lesson, you are on your guard and your reserves of confidence are soon drained. This confidence may be tied to very specific areas of your practice.

Crucially, our belief in our capacity to succeed with each specific aspect of our daily work as teachers is too often characterised as something innate within our character. Like the myth of the 'natural teacher', it can dissuade us from attempting to bolster our own reserves of confidence. Bandura helpfully sweeps away that misnomer by defining the crucial sources from which we develop our authentic confidence.

Bandura argues that there are four essential sources of self-efficacy, and these prove a good basis for our desired teacher confidence:

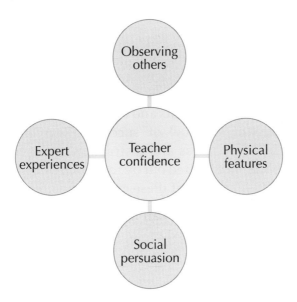

Figure 3.1

Developing self-confidence

Expert experiences

These are experiences when you have been a success. Success nourishes our confidence and we are therefore that little bit better prepared, particularly on an emotional and psychological level, for each subsequent lesson. Each day typically becomes easier as you gain experience, learning from your successes and your many inevitable failures. These marginal gains and tweaks in professional practice amass into a whole that quickly becomes our signature teaching style.

Expert experiences are to be found when you planned and taught a great lesson. Such experiences can arrive unexpectedly in moments within lessons, such as when young Tommy threw off his mask of discontent for one short moment as you successfully explained mathematical division to him. They can be found on the trip to France when young Jude and Claire talked their way out of the local hotel with pitch perfect French, before smiling at you with unfettered pride.

Each positive teaching experience is a fragment from which we build our foundations of self-confidence.

Of course, on tough days we can too easily fritter away our gains. New teachers, seized upon by savvy students, can suffer a series of defeats and failures without anywhere near enough of the fuel of success. Even experienced teachers, beset by stress and distraction, often have their expert experiences blotted out by too much of the opposite.

We need just enough of these expert experiences to beat back our doubts and fears and to sustain us through difficult times. It is crucial that school leaders help create as many of these experiences as possible, shining a light on them when they happen so that we can build a collective catalogue of what works in our classrooms.

Observing others

The experience of watching other teachers do the job expertly is invaluable and seeing other teachers make mistakes can prove just as instructive. Every new teacher gets that precious early period where they get to watch their fellow teachers displaying their craft.

Such observations can be full of subtle revelations. These can be stored, practiced and deployed with intent (but, alas, not always with the same degree of skill). You can mine these observations for gems: the nuanced eye movements that scan the room; the graceful, hidden dance about the class as the students write up their story; a strategic point or a determined stare; an utterly clear explanation of a concept that you had never quite understood yourself.

We should be wary with such observations, though. We are only human. It is harder to observe the most experienced teacher in the school and not feel like we are inferior, meaning many of our observations prove null and void.

We most often learn better when we believe our exemplar is within reach. For students, if they see a great piece of model writing from a friend, whom they feel evenly matched with, then they are likely to have self-confidence that they can do the same. Teachers are no different. Observe the head teacher with a focus on behaviour management and you may be wasting your time. A classroom teacher will never carry the status of the head with students, and it is therefore not a realistic example to follow.

Observing others, in a well-planned manner, can shine a light on great teaching unlike any other method of professional development. It can give us time for reflection and thinking that is all too rare in our hectic working lives. We can see and hear confidence grow and crystallise into practice from such vicarious experiences.

Developing self-confidence

Social persuasion

We share a universal craving for validation from our colleagues and from our boss. The desire is powerful. The impact of a few kind words can resonate deeply. Given a few moments, I'm sure we could each remember an enduring example.

If we trust our colleague speaking to us, then praise and constructive feedback can prove equally as nourishing. It can sometimes lack the impact of fully experiencing success ourselves, but it is still important. Honest praise reaches deep within us and it lingers and replenishes us when we are bashed by bad days in the classroom.

Most teachers have had a teacher in their time as a student who made them feel capable of anything. Often, I hear of teachers inspired to teach by such a character. We shouldn't lose that persuasive magic when we work with our colleagues.

Physical features

Picture a familiar scene: a typical school hall. One hundred teachers sit in their huddled masses on the first day of term. The hubbub of holiday stories passes between friends before quiet descends.

Consider the scenario: you are up to speak in front of all your teacher colleagues.

How do you feel?

Does your heartbeat race? Do your hands clam up as you subtly rock with nervous energy? Beyond the natural fear, you have a decision to make. Is this physical reaction so unbearable that you never want to stand up like this again, or is the adrenaline that is coursing through you something you can manage and help drive you on?

Do you interpret this moment as one characterised by excitement or fear?

Excitement and fear are closely aligned during most of our days in teaching. Being in control of our teacher confidence can see us tread excitedly where others would be paralysed by fear. Such confidence finds a purpose in clammy hands and a surge of adrenaline.

How we interpret these physical signals and how we bear our physicality with others is essential in developing our confidence and expertise as a teacher. In any classroom, in front of a class full of students, our physical self and our physical 'act of confidence' matters a great deal.

What are the obstacles to becoming a self-confident teacher?

It all sounds so easy: learn from some great teachers, teach some great lessons, and be told how great we are, before basking in the glow of excitement. However, that is only in theory. The practice is invariably much tougher.

There is the implication that most teachers, as they get more experienced, would inevitably grow more confident and competent. Most teachers have more than a decade of experience. Surely, then, the opportunities to experience success and to watch other great teachers exhibit their craft are legion. Authentic teacher confidence awaits.

Well, unfortunately not. First, becoming a competent and confident teacher isn't a linear process. Teaching, and developing as a teacher, like most learning, is messy. Our sense of confidence waxes and wanes along with our changing circumstances. We need only suffer an extended absence from work, or change schools, to see our confidence fall away.

Developing self-confidence

Successes can be squeezed from our memory by failures. Selfish leaders and careless rogues can too quickly replace wise guides and supportive colleagues.

The drivers of self-confidence meet with the following roadblocks:

Major issue 1: The problem with student behaviour

Teaching can actually prove an acutely private role. After our training, and aside from a few observations annually, teachers most often teach alone in their classrooms. Now, this can prove empowering if it allows for a free development of your craft, but left unsupported it can prove damaging.

A recent international OECD TALIS[1] survey of teachers revealed that the biggest factor that damaged teacher self-confidence was student misbehaviour. It is the factor that unites a global workforce of millions. It smashes through national boundaries and can wreck learning in classrooms.

Stress and struggle in the classroom is a universal language. I love *Dead Poet's Society* as much as the next teacher of English literature, but the mere thought of my students actually standing on their desks would likely prove a health-and-safety nightmare.

Few teachers, even great teachers heralded for their craft, have not experienced the humbling and crushing experience of losing control of a class. It is chastening and perhaps the biggest influence on those teachers who, drained of all confidence, leave our profession.

Student misbehaviour can too often be a damaging and secret affair. We often dare not share this truth with our more trusted colleagues, much less senior staff, who can often make the biggest difference in helping repair the damage. Even in good schools, with supportive leadership and solid behaviour management systems, this secret battle is being played out behind closed doors.

School leaders at all levels need to shift from a culture of secret struggle and open the doors on our negative behaviour experiences, otherwise the steady stream of good teachers, who could go on to become expert teachers, will continue to flow out of the classroom door and away from teaching altogether.

Major issue 2: The wrong type of observation

Too many nations are creating school systems that foster distrust and accountability measures that become a noose around the most committed of teachers' necks. Instead of opportunities to learn from observing peers, we are thrust into high-stakes observations that become loathed and are functionally useless in helping teachers develop their expertise and their self-confidence.

In cultures driven by a corrosive managerialism, lessons become graded despite the evidence that shows we have great trouble in doing so with even the merest semblance of accuracy. Even the wisest amongst us exhibit a fleet of biases: we regress to the mean and avoid giving the top and bottom grades; we rate teachers in our own school better than others; we develop positive impressions of teachers, which then influences all future ratings (surely the converse is true too).[2] The flaws in such graded observations go on.

In short, as the very expensive Bill and Melinda Gates' research showed, you are pretty much better off tossing a coin than bargaining on the accuracy of a single school leader grading a lesson observation.

Now, this is something most of us can do nothing to change, but in my view knowledge is power. We can challenge bad practice when it comes to observing teachers, and we can shine a light on better practice elsewhere.

In Japan, by stark contrast, they have an established culture of *jugyokenkyuu,* translated as 'lesson study' or 'research lesson'. This sees teachers work in groups to closely observe a lesson with a given focus. This is followed by rich, collaborative talk and reflection on their findings.

Time, collaboration and reflection are the requisite tools to help teachers improve and develop their confidence. Remember Bandura's second source of teacher confidence: observing others.

The Japanese education system exemplifies many important qualities that can happily promote the conditions for teacher confidence. Personal qualities, such as humility and a deep sense of commitment to sharing and improving with others, can be nurtured and grown in such an environment.

There are honourable exceptions. Forward-thinking schools are going to great lengths to change their culture. From removing arbitrary graded judgements of lesson observations, to using video equipment to provide a trusted lens on great teaching, a positive culture of observing teachers can be cultivated.

Many schools are seizing the opportunity to harness an 'open door' culture of lesson observations. Schools are building classrooms with viewing galleries or using video technology to reveal best practice. Some of the most powerful experiences for a teacher can be to watch themselves back on video, with a supportive colleague, peeling back each nuanced layer of the lesson. Our classrooms needn't be secretive bunkers if we use the right technology to shine a light on what we do.

Such pioneering methods can breed confidence, getting teachers talking openly about their teaching mistakes, failures and successes. In such a culture, teachers can lose that inhibiting sense of isolation and can find collective confidence in the support of one another.

Ask yourself: how many times have you observed a colleague solely for continuous professional development? What did you gain from it?

School leaders, and the decisions they make about an observation culture, can prove a key factor in helping teachers develop their expertise and their confidence. Given teacher quality is so crucial, it is remarkable that every school leader doesn't make this priority number one. Evidence would suggest that not all school leaders do so. We need to replace George Orwell's 'Big Brother' culture with that of true sibling-like support.

School programmes like 'lesson study', and even simply having small creases of time for reflection given to us to step off the fast train of the working day, can prove a boon for new teachers and experienced teachers alike.

Major issue 3: The thief of time

Hours can pass in the school day like a hurtling movie montage. Some days you can barely come up for air outside of lessons, meeting students, staff meetings, some marking, data inputting, planning and the obligatory pit stop for lunch.

Every measure points to the worrying increase in teacher workload. The problem is a global one. The evidence shows that in many countries, teachers are working in excess of fifty hours per week. In the US, a report by Scholastic and the Bill and Melinda Gates Foundation,[3] in 2012, found that teachers were reporting working fifty-three hours a week on average. In the UK, the British Secretary of State for Education, Nicky Morgan, has admitted, 'Too many of you are still struggling under the burden of an unnecessary and unsustainable workload.'[4]

Countless reports reiterate the same message: many teachers are overworked. The results of professional burnout can be very damaging for our self-confidence. There are unsurprising links between the emotional exhaustion associated with teachers being overworked and the damage to our sense of confidence and resilience in the face of inevitable daily stresses and failures.[5]

Once more, we may feel powerless in the face of school-wide decision-making, or even national decision-making, but we can promote best practice even if we are stuck in an unhelpful context. We can even make personal decisions that steal back some of our time without compromising our professionalism.

How can we begin to develop our confidence?

It is very easy, in the face of stark statistics about teacher dropout rates, teacher workload increases and stories of demoralised teachers in schools the world over, to throw our arms up in despair.

How, with these conditions, can we not just survive, but see our professional confidence thrive?

Of course, school leadership matters. Even in the worst school systems, school leaders still prove themselves as great leaders by resisting the madness that attends narrow accountability measures, an obsession with standardised testing and debilitating cuts to school budgets.

We can seek to control our own destiny by focusing intently on developing our own confidence and expertise. The place to start is tackling the obstacles head-on and seeking out solutions:

Solution 1: Speak up about your problems

The damaging secret of student misbehaviour is hidden away in every staffroom. We need to remove the stigma and be honest when classes and individual students are misbehaving. First, seek out teachers who have the self-same class, or a similar mix of problematic students. Talk to them and tease out their strategies and swap stories. Encourage your colleagues to do the same.

If behaviour management systems are not fit for purpose, build a collection of voices to bring the problem to light. This can be framed positively, by providing potential solutions that would alleviate the issues. Shine a light on other schools that have found a more effective remedy for the deficit. Share resources, articles and wider views from beyond the school. In short, aim to manage upwards and make changes when they are required.

Of course, we should aim to develop our own behaviour management strategies until they are crystallised into something like confident expertise. Chapter 9 (Managing student behaviour) focuses exclusively on developing our confidence in this essential aspect of our work.

Solution 2: Get social

Many of the most successful schools harness the power of networks, both formally and informally. They are outward looking and they connect to other schools: experts are linked to fellow experts. The best leaders find that successful departments or faculties have cultivated their own unique methods that lead to success. These clusters of excellence harness social learning and can breed a collective confidence.

They develop schemes of learning together, share resources, and observe one another, thereby helping one another negotiate the stresses and workload of each day in a healthy way. School leaders would do well to shine a light on these bright spots so that every network in the school can learn from them and develop.

Of course, these collaborative, richly stimulating networks and departments are not available for us all. No matter. The power of networks now reaches beyond physical boundaries. We have the power of the Internet to help sustain us. Social networking now offers us the opportunity to share and learn outside of our schools. Resources, ideas, evidence, support and more are at our instant touch. Personally, I have found a wealth of resources and ideas scrolling down my Twitter feed and connecting with like-minded teachers.

School programmes for ongoing professional development can often prove inadequate. The ingredients of great professional learning include a sustained focus on professional learning for well over two terms,[6] when too many schools still focus on single-day quick fixes. The best professional learning takes into account the needs of the teacher and the outcomes of their students, but lots of schools still bring in experts who have little knowledge and understanding of the school context.

Teachers can right this state of affairs by supplementing their learning with some DIY.

The international OECD TALIS study is once more instructive. It shows that teachers develop their confidence when they collaborate with fellow teachers. We can seek out critical friends or coaches, both formally and informally. We can tap into the broad seam of social networking for collaboration.

Such networks adapt and grow, meet and greet. Physical TeachMeets and virtual meetings can help us share our woes and successes, whilst dividing the load of planning and preparation. Ultimately, if it proves lacking in our school setting, we can seize control of our own professional learning, making it truly continuous.

Solution 3: Create your own observation culture

Great teaching is all around us. Ideally, our school leaders foster expertise by creating structures for the effective sharing of our best work, but this isn't always the case.

If this is true of your school, then once more, we can share the best of what other schools do. We can share with our school leaders the technologies and methodologies employed by those schools that undertake 'lesson study' and utilise video technology, observation rooms, open door days and more.

We can expose bad practice related to grading lesson observations and destructive 'Big Brother' cultures at large in schools. We can use evidence to shine a light on the folly of grading lessons and similar.

We can encourage an observation culture in our own departments and faculty teams. It may be a simple ten-minute lesson starter, or a weekly slot for reciprocal visits to lessons. It needn't be time intensive. Laborious pro formas can be burnt at the altar of managerialism. Instead, we can talk and share and improve.

Solution 4: Think confidently

The quotation 'they can because they think they can', from the classic poet Virgil, is one of those quotations that has seamlessly translated from its epic Roman origins to now adorn a million motivational posters. It has endured because it is rooted in an age-old human experience common for us all: success nourishes us and gives us confidence.

And yet, asking you to simply begin thinking about your teaching with confidence, without action, will likely prove naïve and foolish. Conversely, possessing an authentic confidence and taking a considered course of action will likely enhance your chances of success, or at the least, help you cope better with failure.

It is easy to be crushed under the weight of hulking great school systems and school leaders who beat our confidence into submission. We must, crucially, believe in our individual agency: that we can individually change our lot, even in the most trying circumstances. Yes – school leaders and even education policymakers can help foster the conditions for teacher growth and confidence, but ultimately, it is each individual teacher that thinks and works their way to confident expertise.

We can resist the alluring draw of easy cynicism. We should be mindful of our confidence and skills in each situation in the working day. Like Albert Bandura, we can rise beyond the limitations of our circumstance, imposing our will and developing our skill.

When I consider the basis of authentic confidence, what lingers in my mind is the story of Albert Bandura's parents. Their hardy shifting of rubble and homemaking is a lifetime away from my experience, but their determination and sheer act of will clearly carved a path for their children of nourishing self-confidence. With effort and support, we can do the same for ourselves and for our students.

IN SHORT...

- The notion of teacher confidence promoted in this chapter can be encapsulated thus: *if you think you can teach, or you think you can't, you are probably right.*
- Teachers face major obstacles to develop their confidence and expertise. These include: student misbehaviour, a damaging observation culture and scarcity of time. Yet, these obstacles can, and are, overcome daily by many teachers.
- When we break down aspects of our daily practice self-critically, and with honesty, we start to identify the specific actions that we need to focus upon on our path to confident expertise.

- We must be proactive, asking questions and seeking out solutions ourselves. We can get social, seeking out positive observations, speaking up and speaking out. We can celebrate our successes and seek out critical friends.
- Confidence in ourselves is the solid keystone for our confidence in our students and their capacity to succeed. Yes – the best laid plans of mice and teachers most often go awry. Even when we think we can succeed we often fail, but possessing an authentic confidence can better sustain us through such failure and give us the necessary fuel for self-improvement.

Notes

1   OECD (2014), 'New insights from TALIS 2013: Teaching and learning in primary and upper secondary education', OECD Publishing. [Online]. Available at: http://dx.doi.org/10.1787/9789264226319-en (Accessed: 5 February 2015).
2   Ho, A.D. and Kane, T.J. (2013), 'The reliability of classroom observations by school personnel', MET Project Research Paper, Bill and Melinda Gates Foundation.
3   'Primary sources: 2012 America's teachers on the teaching profession' (2012), A project of Scholastic and the Bill and Melinda Gates Foundation. [Online]. Available at: http://mediaroom.scholastic.com/files/ps_fullreport.pdf (Accessed: 10 May 2015).
4   Morgan, N., TES Opinion (2014) 'Nicky Morgan: I want to build a new deal for teacher workload – and I need your help'. [Online]. Available at: www.tes.com/news/school-news/breaking-views/nicky-morgan-'i-want-build-a-new-deal-teacher-workload---and-i-need (Accessed: 21 October 2014).
5   Skaalvik, E.M. and Skaalvik, S. (2010), 'Teacher self-efficacy and teacher burnout: A study of relations', Teaching and Teacher Education 26: 1059–1069.

Developing self-confidence

6   The Teacher Development Trust (2015), 'Developing great teaching: Lessons from the international reviews into effective professional development'. [Online]. Available at: http://tdtrust.org/wp-content/uploads/2015/06/Developing-Great-Teaching-Summary.pdf (Accessed: 5 June 2015).

4 The pursuit of expertise

There exists no more difficult art than living. For other arts and sciences, numerous teachers are to be found everywhere.

Seneca

Understanding our own psychology, our character traits and our varying degrees of confidence, is no easy task. Since the dawn of Western thought, crystallised in the thing we call philosophy, there has been a recognition that it is perhaps the most difficult thing in life – *even* harder than herding children on a windy lunchtime.

The art of living, and teaching, is difficult. So much so, that making real sustainable improvements to our professional lives and our practice in the classroom takes not weeks, nor months, but years of challenging, hard work. We all can fall for the enticement of the speedy habit fix, the quick fad diet, the annual parade of self-deception that is the January gym membership surge...but they won't work.

These self-help staples rely on our mistaken notion that we all require a complete transformation. Instead, as Oliver Burkeman recommends in his excellent book, *Help!*, we should ignore advice, fads or books that 'exude perfectionism' and instead focus on 'just getting a bit better'. The stress that attends the unattainable goal of perfection is simply wasted energy.

How liberating is the thought that we will never be the *perfect teacher*? We can end the agonising strain of aiming to be better than our peers. Instead, we can aim to be the best version of ourselves – and just a little bit better at that. It is a goal that proves more achievable, breeding hope.

The success of a career in education (you can substitute education for pretty much any career) was not founded on a momentary stare in the mirror to announce your own greatness. Nor was it purchased for a tidy sum on a gloss-laden course at a nondescript hotel. Becoming a successful and confident teacher is founded upon thousands of small, incremental actions and habits.

So, if we ignore the potentially crippling effects of aiming to be a perfect teacher, is it okay to be simply 'okay'? Well, not really. Let me explain.

In his excellent popular science book, *Moonwalking with Einstein*, Joshua Foer, coined the term the 'ok plateau'. He used it to describe that common state of being on autopilot: when you have habitually mastered the basics of a given task, but once you acquire skills that are okay or passable, you begin to plateau in performance. We shouldn't be surprised when the evidence shows[1] that teacher quality can plateau, regardless of our deepening experience, as we become time poor and we lack the intensity of coaching and support that characterises our initial teacher training.

There is a hoary old proverb, passed on from teacher to teacher. It goes something like this: *some teachers have twenty years of experience in the classroom, others have one year of experience twenty times.* In this case, perhaps staffroom wisdom should be heeded.

The notion of this plateau in our performance has always stuck with me as pertinent for teachers. I recognised that I crashed into the 'ok plateau' quite early in my career and I wallowed in it, unknowingly, for some time. After a couple of years or so I had grasped a basic competence in the essentials: behaviour management, feedback and the nuts and bolts of the curriculum. Rarely was I coached like a novice any more. My habits quickly hardened into my teaching identity: Mr Quigley.

It wasn't simply from a lack of effort. I was trying to get 'just a little bit better', but it simply wasn't working out very well. It shouldn't come as a grand surprise. Simply repeating an action doesn't necessarily improve it. In fact, it can have the opposite effect. Unintentionally, we can entrench mistakes deeply within the very grain of how we work.

Without skilful coaching, or timely and continuous training tailored to our needs, we seldom get better at what we do. We should remember the seemingly obvious point that teaching is a process of learning and therefore we should mirror the best of how our students learn with how we expect teachers to learn and improve.

Would we expect our students to be successful if we taught them for a few days a year and provided few other supports?

A common motivational inspiration from my past, one that encapsulates the world of self-improvement, is the leaping pose of Michael Jordan. His other-worldly basketball expertise led to unparalleled career success, financial endorsements and a slew of motivational posters. Famously, he declared that his success came from his failure, or more specifically, from his failure in missing some 9000 shots.

Now, I can't shoot a basketball very well either, but I have surely miskicked at least 9000 footballs and, alas, I still cannot stake a claim to footballing greatness. So what is the difference? Like almost all experts, he conquered his many failures, and he had a hell of a lot of top class coaching at just the right time in his development.

Akin to Michael Jordan, teachers require high-quality coaching and training. Every school leader and politician that steers education policy, should concentrate upon improving continuous teacher development and learning if they want better teaching for our ultimate aim: improved outcomes for our students.

After a year or so learning the classroom ropes – my personal 'rope-a-dope' strategy (Muhammad Ali infamously took a beating from George Foreman before bouncing back with panache to win the day) was pretty much all dope and no rope – but I wasn't the only one. Most teachers survive the initial onslaught of the first year before being plunged headlong into the classroom with a few intermittent training sessions. Of course, these are not the conditions in which we best pursue expertise.

Becoming an expert teacher isn't merely repeating your teaching habits over and over. The process of becoming a confident teacher expert is much more nuanced than turning up and repeating the cycle of school terms with the switch set to autopilot. It requires time, trusted relationships, high-quality training and support, alongside our will and passion to keep on taking our shots, even when we miss.

The wisdom of practice

So what habits and strategies should we practise to conquer the 'ok plateau'? Alas, the answers don't come quick and easy. Bill Gates, of Microsoft fame, argues that:

> *Unfortunately, it seems the field doesn't have a clear view of what characterises good teaching.*[2]

What if I told you, after exhaustive research, that I agreed with Bill and that there was no easy answer to what good teaching is and what therefore characterises an expert teacher? It would certainly be something of a damp squib for this book. Luckily, Bill is only half-right. By studying expertise as a process and by studying teaching as a craft *and* an art *and* a science, we can find something of a working guide to becoming an expert teacher. By combining the nuances of subject expertise with the best of *how* to teach, we can capture something like teacher expertise.

So, the questions should be: what do we know about teaching expertise and how do we get it?

Of course, there is no one singular answer to teacher expertise, or the pursuit of confidence. Lee Shulman, American educational psychologist, in his excellent paper, 'The Wisdom of Practice', captured this complexity brilliantly with his description:

> *After 30 years of doing such work, I have concluded that classroom teaching...is perhaps the most complex, most challenging, and most demanding, subtle, nuanced, and frightening activity that our species has ever invented.*

He went on to compare the classroom to 'the emergency room of a hospital during or after a natural disaster.'[3]

The teacher as a physician in an emergency room in a hospital is an arresting image. Lee clearly must have secretly observed some of my teaching. This accurate depiction of the maddening and brilliant complexity of the classroom goes some way to explaining why there is no easily defined formula for an expert teacher, or even good teaching, as Bill Gates states.

Indeed, the very notion of expertise resists such a formulaic approach, but it doesn't defy us taking a working method that we can practise and hone.

The expert teacher applies a range of subtle skills with confidence. They are simply that bit better than your average teacher in many small but significant ways. Each small improvement aggregates and becomes what we define as expertise. Such teachers are flexible; they problem-solve and problem-seek; they filter quickly for important information; they integrate and improvise with their specific subject content at the point that students receive it.[4]

Expert teachers have good subject knowledge, but they have even better knowledge of the subject knowledge of their students. This is a subtle but crucial difference. They weave patterns of meaning and unpick patterns for students caught up in misunderstanding. If we could distil this expertise we can all move closer to becoming competent and confident teachers.

The 'moves' of an expert teacher

A good starting point in defining a confident teacher expert comes from our good friend Albert Bandura:

> *Let us not confuse ourselves by failing to recognize that there are two kinds of self-confidence—one a trait of personality and another that comes from knowledge of a subject. It is no particular credit to the educator to help build the first without building the second. The objective of education is not the production of self-confident fools.[5]*

With every story of experts in their field, there is evidence of the confidence that attends deep, often hard-earned knowledge. Self-confident fools they are not.

Let's consider some of those stories of experts in their field, at a distance from teaching.

The life of the Cuban, José Raúl Capablanca, is well known to his many adoring fans; however, only a small proportion of people reading this book are likely to recognise his unique expertise. José became famous as a chess grandmaster, considered by many as the greatest *natural* chess player of all time.

He learnt the game of chess at the age of four, watching his father play and correcting him in what was surely an act of ignorant bravery. José developed into a chess expert – not losing a game in the span between 1916 and 1924. He became known affectionately as the 'human chess machine'.

José proudly declared he had never read a book on chess. His skill and expertise was honed through intense deliberate practice. His quick-paced play was testimony to his phenomenal knowledge of thousands of chess moves and their accompanying sequences of intricate moves and counter moves. To describe him as a *natural* does a disservice to these thousands of hours of deliberate play and improvement.

Now, here is another non-teaching expert. Nicknamed the 'Oracle of Omaha', Warren Buffett is widely considered to be one of the greatest financial investors of all time. He is likely better known than José, but his incredible expertise in the financial markets makes him an even match with the chess grandmaster and an intriguing example of instruction for teachers looking to get better at what they do.

Why is Warren Buffett such an investment expert in a field often reduced to guesswork? His succinct response: 'I just sit in my office and read all day.' He estimates that he spends at least 80 per cent of his time thinking and reading. Like a chess player, he scrutinises the fast-paced 'moves' in the financial markets.

Both these experts, to my knowledge, have never stepped into a classroom to teach, but their degree of confident expertise is instructive. They knew their subject intimately: chess and financial investment respectively.

How both take a complex wealth of information and cohere it into patterns, whilst making their decisions in tough situations, drawing upon a tremendous depth of knowledge, should make us think. We too must have a deep knowledge of our subject/s, as well as a rich knowledge of how students learn, if we are to become teaching experts.

Interestingly, José Raúl Capablanca and Warren Buffett conducted a different approach to practice. José apparently rejected studying other grandmasters (except in the flesh) or reading about the game for repeated game practice, whereas Warren studiously read and built up his theoretical knowledge before conducting his 'moves'. For teachers, we too need to find that subtle balance between practice in the classroom alongside reflection and reading outside the classroom. The white heat of action needs to be cooled by the waters of reflection.

So were Warren and José born with a unique genius? The role of genetics will likely play a significant part in their capacity to become experts in their field, but the common observation we can make is that they devoted a huge amount of their professional lives to deliberate, and sometimes downright difficult, practice.

As teachers we cannot alter our students' genetic inheritance, but we can create fertile conditions for practice that can help them develop. Similarly, we can alter our habits and create our own conditions for professional growth. By committing to learning the moves of their respective 'game', Warren and José, after thousands of hours, were able to note complex patterns of behaviours and respond successfully.

There is the 'game' of the classroom. It involves moves like asking great questions, giving feedback, explaining new concepts, managing each small but significant student behaviour, and much more. Expertise, and confidence, emerges when a teacher has practised each element of the game so that our understanding becomes something like automatic, but then we consciously fend off any plateau with considered critical reflection.

Dr K Anders Ericsson, probably *the* expert in the field of expertise, has defined such 'game practice' as *deliberate practice*. That is to say, the process of breaking down a complex skill into its component parts – the *moves*. These sharply defined moves – like the process of asking open questions in the classroom; or filing into the class in an orderly fashion as a lesson begins – are honed by repeated practice. Crucially, though, it is not just unthinking repetition. This practice is then met with specific feedback – ideally in the form of an expert coach, but not exclusively so.

Such a process requires a high degree of commitment. Crucially, it requires a good amount of self-confidence to see one through the challenges and inevitable failures of such repeated practice. It requires effort, commitment and self-confidence to delve into the process of self-reflection required to make genuine improvements to what we do each day. It takes intelligence to understand the minutiae of marginal improvement.

In effect, each expert, like each teacher undergoing training, undertakes the mental process of 'chunking' when taking part in such practice. This is a process whereby information is clustered into smaller more manageable chunks. It is essential to how we think and to help us function, particularly in dynamic contexts like the classroom.

To give an example, try to memorize this telephone number: 0789554938.

How did you go about the process? Most people instinctively chunk the information into component parts that are more easily manageable and memorable. I went for 0 – 789 – 554 – 938.

By this method, entire patterns of stock market behaviour, chess play and classroom practice can be processed into more manageable parts. This is often undertaken as an unconscious process. People paint such experts as 'naturals', when the reality is that they have committed hours and hours of deliberate practice. Like José, they become machine-like, though I dare not offer the notion of the 'Teaching Machine' for fear of dire recriminations from angry teachers.

Seemingly, authentic confidence flows from the wellspring of expertise. Not all experienced teachers are experts of course, but very few experts are inexperienced. The myth of the *gift of genius* too often ignores the conditions in which such 'gifts' were hard earned through practice.

What was once difficult and clumsy – like my first 'disaster zone' lessons – became automatic. A hundred little behaviours and signals from students about their learning became visible. In the midst of those lessons I would be hard-pressed to describe what I knew and where I was making marginal improvements, but it was certainly no 'natural gift' bestowed upon me.

We must actively fend off the lazy stereotyping of the 'natural teacher'. In her book *Building a Better Teacher*, Elizabeth Green captured the essence of teacher expertise when she described a teacher called Magdalene. She described how Magdalene defied the stereotype of the mythic teachers of Hollywood lore. Success was not related to personality like those on the big screen – instead, she is described by Green as quiet and unassuming, but in possession of a deep body of knowledge.

Green goes on to describe teaching as an incredibly complex craft in the same reverent manner of Lee Shulman. She punctures the lazy notion that becoming a confident teacher expert, like Magdalene, is something that emerges from an innate talent or gift.

Whether consciously or unconsciously, Magdalene has gone about chunking down the process of teaching and has developed her own expert pattern of 'moves'. By breaking them down, then structuring them into workable patterns, she has undergone another process attributed to experts – the creation of 'schemas'.

The term is quite simple really. 'Schema' comes from the Greek meaning 'shape', or more generally, the 'plan'. It is effectively the web that connects all the disparate 'moves' together in a coherent pattern. Consider it like a wardrobe: we have our shelves and drawers compartmentalised to organise our clothes so that they are easily accessible. Like new knowledge, we can more easily store it.

Take a moment to consider the different moves in teaching. Here is my basic list (for fear of running out of ink) for any given lesson:

- Subject-specific knowledge of the topic at hand
- Making expectations clear
- The effective explanation of concepts
- Modelling those concepts clearly
- How best to group students during time on task
- When to focus students in on hard thinking
- Asking questions: both simple and complex, open and closed
- Differentiating questions where appropriate
- Behaviour management strategies
- Managing the timing and 'flow' of the lesson
- Reacting to misunderstandings; deviating from the plan when needed

- Checking for student understanding
- Checking the standard of focus and effort is appropriate

The list of 'moves' goes on. You could likely list many more. Now, take the time to compile a fulsome list of your own, before then going about chunking it down. Create your own pattern or even a diagram if it helps. Even better, discuss it with some colleagues.

Experts go one step further. They are able to take their knowledge of the 'moves' and make creative decisions about trialling and combining the 'moves' in practice – even in the relative chaos of the classroom.

Try it yourself. What word connects these three word selections: 'vivid – elephant – lapse'? The answer may prove tricky, but as soon as you hear it you appear confident you knew it all along. This confidence, and creativity, is essentially rooted in deep knowledge.

Expert teachers, akin to Warren Buffett and the investment market, make those creative connections and link the patterns together into schemas quickly and successfully, far beyond small word games. Their knowledge of the 'moves' is so extensive that they can draw upon it at will. The benefits are clear: chunking our teaching moves together, we create energy-saving shortcuts, so valuable for a busy teacher.

Oh, if you wanted the answer to the earlier word association question, the answer is *memory*. This question is one of many from the 'Remote Associations Test' – do an Internet search and find out more.

We need to reflect on our own teaching expertise, or at the very least working out what we don't know (remember the threat posed by overconfidence). Then we can decide upon what marginal aspects of our teaching practice we should isolate and work upon improving.

Taking the time to invest in self-improvement

When I was swimming in a sea of troubles as a novice teacher, frankly it was understandable why. I didn't know how to respond to students when they didn't react as I had expected, or when bad timing – or worse – ruined my lesson plan. Given experience, and the right type of practice, we can better respond to such spontaneous challenges with creativity and with confidence.

Like the doctor in the middle of the emergency zone, we are making instantaneous decisions under pressure. We are readied to respond best by practice, reflection and our confidence, to act. It requires ample time and reflection. Though the amount of time is not so important as the quality of the time we spend, or the deliberateness of what we do.

Unfortunately, a message I will reiterate in this book is that teaching is a thief of time and we will never have enough. Yet, we should be reassured that we can stick at it and find small but crucial creases of time (as explored in Chapter 5: The productive teacher) to reflect, refine and repeat what we do in the classroom.

As I write books about teaching, you may argue that I am grossly biased (that I am), but I strongly believe that we should not just act as teachers – we should continue to read and learn about the theory and action of teaching – no matter how hardened our veteran status.

I plateaued after a few years of teaching and it was reading about teaching, away from the stresses of being at school, which allowed me to stand back and question how I was going about my daily work. Though it cost me time in reading in the short term, I quickly learnt to stop wasting my time with ill-considered activities, and I felt I was gaining time and deepening my knowledge.

We can better reflect in other ways too. As mentioned earlier, with effective school training, such as a whole-school approach to formative feedback, we are in a better position to undertake *deliberate practice*. When did you last stand back and analyse how you teach? When did you last seek out a coach or a critical teacher friend to compare notes? When did you last read deeply about the 'moves' of effective teaching?

We can be struck dumb by simple questions about what we do for hours on end each day. Seemingly easy questions, like 'What do you teach well?' or 'What are your strongest moves?' can trouble us. Self-improvement, and the confidence that attends it, stems from a deep knowledge of our own practice and provides an answer to such questions.

We can always learn how to develop upon our practice, even by observing the expertise of chess players and financial investors.

Planning makes permanent

In the crucible of the classroom, it can be hard to learn anything about what really works and what doesn't. We are constantly evolving our practice, adapting our moves and recognising the full game. Investing our time in planning creates the best conditions for recognising how to best direct ourselves towards expertise.

The time we have as teachers is of course finite and we must prioritise accordingly. One such priority must always be planning. Exactly how much is relative to your degree of knowledge in your subject and the 'moves'.

When I started off as a new teacher many lessons really did teeter on the brink of disaster. My best-laid plans were failing repeatedly, despite taking an age to devise. I couldn't work out why. I couldn't discern a pattern amidst the tangle of student misbehaviour, fudged feedback and blown timings. I couldn't see the big picture of learning and where the individual lessons fell within that sequence. I sought good help from my colleagues and muddled through.

It wasn't for want of effortful planning. Some of my lesson plans were epic in scale. I would script my entire lesson introductions, and planned every minute detail of the lesson as much as I could. In retrospect, it was a frantic attempt to staunch the many wounds in my very own classroom disaster zone.

Over time, such planning becomes rationalised and honed. An expert teacher absorbs the complex past experiences and a detailed script can become a mere shopping list. Each point on the list can prove a prompt for a wealth of mental notes that can be applied flexibly and automatically, even whilst the 'frightening activity' of teaching is in full flow.

To show my lesson plans now to my younger, more desperate, new-teacher self would provide light at the end of the tunnel. I would recommend to my younger self to still complete those more detailed lesson plans, but to be ruthless with shelving the many extraneous jobs that are thieves of my time, such as devising elaborate resources and the like.

The confident teacher hones their planning down to the essentials. They ask the simple but profound question: what do I want my students to really think hard about in this lesson and in this sequence of lessons? From that point, each 'move' must be to that end.

If I am teaching a particular poem in my English class, I would identify the key moves. I would ask myself: what questions should I ask to check for understanding, and to whom should I direct them? What prior knowledge would prove most useful for deep understanding of the poem? What focused writing task would best consolidate their understanding? What common misconceptions should I anticipate? I would aim to deploy a deep knowledge of the content of the poem, with understanding of my students, and how to connect the two with success.

The best-laid plans of the novice and the expert

The difference between the novice – almost always lacking in confidence due to their struggle and failures – and the confident expert is marked in pretty much everything that they do.

John Hattie, in his research on what distinguishes expert teachers from novice teachers, identifies common patterns that mark out confident teacher experts over teachers who could only be described as 'experienced' but lacking true expertise.

Hattie describes how expert teachers 'quickly recognize sequences of events occurring in the classroom.'[6] Due to their greater knowledge of the teaching 'moves', he indicates that expert teachers can better respond to students spontaneously, quickly recognising patterns of miscomprehension and misunderstanding. Experts more flexibly deviate from plans when needed because they can better anticipate, plan and improvise according to the unique needs of their students. They regularly ask good questions and successfully seek out feedback and then swiftly respond to what students need.

Couple these skills with the interesting observation that expert teachers rely on sourcing more precise information about the background, experience and the ability of the students they have taught.

Put simply, expert teachers make better decisions in the busy hubbub of the classroom. Even without a lesson plan, expert teachers could accurately guide you through the learning process with just their mental plans. In the classrooms of expert teachers, students ask more questions and the allowance for student failure is fostered, quickly generating a more accurate knowledge of what exact support the students really need.

Novice teachers stick to the leaden signposts of the curriculum without the mental agility or creativity to adapt. Lesson objectives become life rafts they cling to, whereas experts are busy filtering all the other available information: the prior knowledge of students, their little behaviour cues, the resources at hand, the different teaching strategies, the current crises of life beyond school that are preoccupying their students, and more.

The novice is the chess player thinking one move ahead. The confident expert is visualising the next ten moves down the line and hunting down kings and queens with insights garnered from their previous wins.

The novice, busy grappling with the knowledge of their subject, and its application in the curriculum, is blind to the thousands of student 'moves': their misunderstandings, misapprehensions and moments of brilliant insight. The expert, in contrast, is able to integrate the two into their thinking. A question from a bewildered student is not a blocker, but an opportunity. Indeed, when experts are tasked with taking a new class they are less focused on the content of the curriculum and more interested in finding out about the prior knowledge of their students.[7] By thinking of future moves in the chess game, they place themselves in a better position.

An expert teacher is both a confident problem-solver, as well as being a problem-seeker. With quick, automatic routines, they better recognise the significant events amidst the complexity. They spot when a student is playing up for attention, as opposed to being genuinely stuck in their learning. They can quickly revisit an explanation as they notice the class is flailing with a new concept. They have a new analogy at hand to aid understanding, or they model a necessary process with timely precision.

With the confidence of expertise comes the drive for autonomy. Whereas novice teachers lack the confidence to depart from prescribed lesson plans, the expert teacher recognises failings and digs into their repertoire of routines and strategies, deftly redirecting the flow of the learning. A detailed lesson plan can even prove stifling in this regard.

When I use the word 'flow' I deploy it with specific intent. The psychologist Mihaly Csikszentmihalyi used the term 'flow' to describe the process of learning when you are fully immersed in an activity – a state of seemingly effortless concentration. For expert teachers, they can teach in this state and create the conditions for students to better find their 'flow' too.

I have described already the experience of the novice observing an expert teacher. It can be maddening; such is the seeming effortless nature of the task at hand.

Sadly, no quick solution is to be found. Teaching is far more complex than that and children, too. Still, if we look in the right places we may shine a light on the journey from novice to expert and see what that brings us (also, we should not forget that many novices hit the heights too, whereas even much-vaunted experts can fail).

Ultimately, we should be kind to novice teachers and help remind them that the deck is stacked against them, but that they can and will get better.

Deliberate practice with a little help from our friends

It should come as no surprise that teachers improve when they are given time and the right conditions to grow. And yet, some school leaders prioritise this practice more than others. Those school leaders who give teachers targeted feedback in a climate of trust, alongside time to reflect on their practice, best promote confidence amongst their teaching staff.[8]

Indeed, such school leadership is critical in retaining teachers and can create a sense of collective confidence.

Every expert requires good coaching, with the time to be coached. Sadly, too few governments truly privilege teacher improvement by prioritising such time, so the burden falls upon school leaders to create it wherever possible.

A primary role for school leaders is clearing away unnecessary bureaucracy, such as endless lesson observations, repeated data inputting and recording our every move for the sake of compliance. Instead, school leaders can shield their teachers from endless government diktats and focus more on the primacy of our practice.

In schools that create a strong climate of continuous development, with regular time to focus upon professional practice, teachers can improve at a greater rate than those without a determined focus on deliberate practice.[9] This is plain common sense, but as we know, too often common sense doesn't prove so common.

School leaders have a crucial role here, but like any successful organisation, there is a demand for high-quality leadership from everybody, no matter what role in the school.

Unsurprisingly, expert teachers teaching their peers can grow collective confidence and improve the practice in every classroom in the school. Buddying up new teachers with those who have swung on the ropes for a while is useful, and creating coaching teams and time for sessions when teachers talk about teaching and teach one another is essential too. A buddying system can have a significant impact on teacher confidence and well-being.

In pursuit of teaching expertise

Moving from novice to expert status takes time – there is no getting around that; however, we may better accelerate the process and minimise the disasters along the way.

In short, to become expert teachers we need a complex combination of the following:

69

The pursuit of expertise

1 Deep and well organised subject knowledge
2 Deep knowledge of our students and the strategies to enhance that knowledge
3 Spells of intensive deliberate practice with good coaching feedback
4 Time to reflect upon the complex nuances of our practice in the classroom
5 The confidence and motivation to persevere through difficulties

Points 1 and 2 comprise the deep knowledge we need to acquire before we can reach the confident heights of the teacher expert. Points 3 and 4 overlap and are supported by your school, but you can seek them both out independently, too. Point 5, at the heart of this book, comes with the successful development of each of the four points that precede it in this list.

We can quicken this acquisition of expertise by ensuring that we are continuing to read and research around our subject discipline/s and focusing on the teaching strategies that work best within our subject/s. We must never fall prey to thinking that our learning has stopped. We should be the ultimate role models for continuous learning.

There are many books that delineate effective deliberate practice and support successful teacher coaching, such as *Practice Perfect* or *Teach Like a Champion*, by Doug Lemov, or *Talent is Overrated*, by Geoff Golvin, or *Bounce*, by Matthew Syed, so teachers can take some control of their own development if their school conditions prove barren.

In his research for his widely read book, *Teach Like a Champion*, Doug Lemov observed a great number of teacher experts and unpicked their ingrained habits. When he shared their moves with others he found they admired them but struggled to replicate them. There was a wide gap between understanding and being able to execute these moves. Until he began using practice as part of training, that is. What Doug observed was even a little practice helped teachers be much more effective in both using and expanding what they knew: 'Practice is one of the best – and often least used – ways to develop knowledge about teaching.'

Lemov recommends the power of meaningful practice that eschews novelty and gimmicks: 'We've all been in this situation. We are speaking to our class and we give the directions or phrase the question or ask the student to pay attention not quite right. We wish we had another chance to shift the language or the tone slightly, but we don't. We're live in the classroom and our interactions are one-and-done. Practice changes all that.'

Lemov goes on to describe how teachers pursue expertise: 'I choose a common interaction – asking my class to come to order, say – and practice it. Each time I rehearse, I move the tone and the words closer to "just right" and closer to fluid so they come out that way, automatically, while I am teaching. Perhaps I even practice with a colleague and she gives me feedback: "Try it calmer and slower, maybe so you don't sound nervous. Drop your voice a little."'

It is this careful, nuanced reflection and deliberate practice that sees teachers hone their moves towards expertise, just like the human chess machine and the 'Oracle of Omaha'. Such practice is hard and beset by failure, but each failure moves us forward a step.

Matthew Syed, in *Bounce*, describes a paradox of expert performance: failure is essential. Moving beyond one's comfort zone and recognising the boundaries of what is possible is needed to gain real expertise. Schools, and teachers, must therefore embrace risk and failure. If we want better teachers, and therefore better schools, governments and policymakers need to take note.

It may take time to establish all of these links and combining the necessary 'moves', but ultimately, over time, you will reap the rewards of attaining expertise and all the time and pain that is saved by reaching such a professional peak.

For much more on the specific *'moves'* of expert teaching, you can read **Section 3** on **Confident Pedagogy.'**

IN SHORT...

- If we waited to be confident in our every action, we would likely never make a start on anything, much less something as challenging as teaching. We must, after some judicious looking, go and leap.
- There is no quick fix to becoming an expert in anything, let alone teaching. Becoming a confident and competent teacher will require a great deal of challenging deliberate practice, with failure proving as common an experience as success.
- Those teachers, bolstered by the fuel of self-confidence, will learn from failure and better persist toward expertise.
- Confident teachers don't look to transform themselves. Instead, they are practical and pragmatic, aiming for small, marginal improvements. They break down the 'moves' of the teaching 'game', recognising patterns before chunking them together to create tangible improvements in their practice.

Notes

1 Rivkin, S.G., Hanushek, E.A. and Kain, J.F. (2005), 'Teachers, schools, and academic achievement', *Econometrica* 73 (2): 417–458.
2 Gates, B. (2015), 'Bill Gates – A forum on education in America', Prepared remarks by Bill Gates, co-chair and trustee. [Online]. Available at: www.gatesfoundation.org/

media-center/speeches/2008/11/bill-gates-forum-on-education-in-america (Accessed: 6 February 2015).

3   Thomasian, M. (2007), 'The wisdom of practice: Essays on teaching, learning, and learning to teach, by Lee S. Shulman'. *Journal of Catholic Education*, 11 (2). [Online]. Available at: http://digitalcommons.lmu.edu/ce/vol11/iss2/12 (Accessed: 5 May 2015).

4   Hattie, J. (2003), 'Teachers make a difference: What is the research evidence?' University of Auckland, Australian Council for Educational Research. [Online]. Available at: http://growthmindseteaz.org/files/RC2003_Hattie_TeachersMakeADifference_1_.pdf (Accessed: 3 January 2015).

5   Bandura, A. (1997), *Self Efficacy: The Exercise of Control*, p 6. New York: W.H. Freeman and Company.

6   Hattie, J. (2003), 'Teachers make a difference: What is the research evidence?' Australian Council for Educational Research Annual Conference on: Building Teacher Quality. [Online]. Available at: https://cdn.auckland.ac.nz/assets/education/hattie/docs/teachers-make-a-difference-ACER-(2003).pdf (Accessed: 3 March 2015).

7   Livingston, C. and Borko, H. (1989), 'Expert-novice differences in teaching: A cognitive analysis and implications for teacher education', *Journal of Teacher Education*, 40: 36–42.

8   Waters, J.T., Marzano, R.J. and McNulty, B. (2004), 'Leadership that sparks learning', *Educational Leadership*, 61 (7): 48–52.

9   Kraft, M.A. and Papay, J.P. (2014), 'Can professional environments in schools promote teacher development? Explaining heterogeneity in returns to teaching experience'. *Educational Effectiveness and Policy Analysis*, 36 (4): 476–500.

5 The productive teacher

Anthony Trollope was one of the most successful novelists of the Victorian age. A role model of relentless productivity, he awoke daily at 5:30am and wrote a thousand words an hour. He would go on to write forty-nine novels in thirty-five years, each composed before the school bell rings in the morning.

Trollope famously lauded his daily habits and rituals as the basis for his ridiculously prolific output. He remarked: 'A small daily task, if it be really daily, will beat the labours of a spasmodic Hercules.'[1]

It is a simple, but difficult code to live and work by, but perhaps it is the ideal advice for teachers.

The patron saint of teaching

Teaching can often take the patience and persistence of a saint. St Expeditus fits the bill for our new patron saint nicely (sorry St John Baptist de La Salle).

Like most saints, St Expeditus has an oddly illuminating biography. A Roman centurion of repute, his legend relates his dramatic and swift conversion to Christianity. The devil, shape-shifting in the guise of a crow, attempted to caw Expeditus into putting off his decision to convert his faith, calling angrily to him 'tomorrow, tomorrow'. In heroic defiance, Expeditus stomped on the devil-bird with a victorious shout of 'today!' In an instant, he became the patron saint of procrastinators, and teachers, everywhere.

With apologies to bird lovers, we should remember that image of the devil-crow stomping saint. Of course, the devilish power of procrastination is living and thriving in us all still.

Beyond saintly narratives, we have characters like the Greek poet, Hesiod – back in 800 BC – lambasting procrastinators for putting off their work until tomorrow. He had in mind sluggish farm workers not filling their barn. The filling of the barn could easily prove a metaphor for teachers straining to write reports, communicate with parents, plan and teach their lessons, whilst marking students' work, attending meetings and the rest, all in a single day.

You see, centuries pass, but human nature doesn't change a great deal. Teenagers will be demonised, teachers likely overworked, and procrastination will continue to taint us all.

As Parkinson's Law states: work will expand to fill the time available. Teachers are particularly bound by this law. Teacher workload across the world is on the increase, with technology penetrating every boundary of our lives with work.

Now, St Expeditus lived in a bygone age, but our capacity to procrastinate in the present is as strong as ever. In a world of instant communication, it is hard to do what is truly important and not what is simply urgent. It can prove stressful and difficult to recognise the difference. The work of a teacher appears to now seep into every part of our lives, with little ability to switch off seemingly urgent demands.

There are legions of reasons that can attend our procrastination. Some are deeply set emotional barriers, like an avoidance of failure, or a fear of the negative judgement of others. A confident and assured teacher is forced to manage these emotional barriers daily. Other reasons include the curse of perfectionism, where we can never finish anything because nothing meets our unrealistic standards.

The best advice I have been given, by a wise school leader, is: the day that you realise you will never do the job perfectly is the day you can start enjoying and flourishing in your working life. It worked for me, so it may help you too.

The to-do list of a teacher is invariably like Mary Poppins' bag: endlessly deep and sometimes just as mysterious. The image of the tortured genius, poring over their work obsessively, should not be our yardstick. Nor are we perfect, like the saintly singing nanny. We must face the fact that cutting corners and compromising upon perfection is simply the lived daily experience of *every* teacher. Admitting this can prove a blessed relief.

There is plain laziness that can result in procrastination of course, although in my experience this is a rare trait in a teacher. The job simply doesn't tolerate the idle for long.

With a job that is so multifaceted and complex, it can prove a challenge to know where to start, but with better organisation and improved time management, we can find ourselves more confidently managing our job. We can make small improvements to our working day that free up creases of time to then develop our practice.

It is time we started exercising some strategies to help us to confidently trample the devilish crows of procrastination with St Expeditus.

Teaching: Taking our time

There are entire books written about organisation and time management. Sadly, with bitter-tasting irony, you probably don't have time to read them. With that in mind, this chapter aims to give you some workable strategies to better manage your time and allow you some freedom and time to grow your confidence.

First, we need to be clear that we do have different types of time in our working day. We have our *fixed time* and our *fluid time.*

By fixed time I mean the core aspects of the job that are scheduled in and are not subject to change. Our teaching timetable is of course our predominant quota of fixed time. Regular meetings would come under fixed time too.

This time is largely out of our control. Of course, the less say we have over our time management, the harder it can be to manage, so teachers with the heaviest teaching hours allocated to them invariably find themselves struggling the most.

Fluid time, by contrast, is relatively flexible, and though we have to complete it, the *how* and *when* is more within our control and on our terms. Alas, we have too little fluid time and too much of our time is fixed, but we must concentrate upon what we can better control.

Many aspects of teaching, like lesson planning and giving written feedback, often move between both fluid and fixed time definitions. If we do them well, concisely, without any unnecessary excesses, then we can go a long way to making our working week manageable.

We therefore need to think and plan most carefully with our fluid time. It can encompass a wealth of jobs, such as:

- Lesson planning
- Giving feedback on students' work
- Finding or creating lesson resources
- Inputting data
- Impromptu meetings
- Observing colleagues teaching
- Responding to emails
- Reading up on best practice
- Communicating with parents

That is little more than a snapshot of some core actions undertaken by a teacher on a daily basis. I could fill a book with a full list of fluid time tasks for teachers. A helpful approach is to take a *time audit* over the course of your teaching week. Focus on the actions that you consider to be fluid and time yourself as you go. It is an inconvenience in the short term, no doubt, but it will give you a valuable insight into your working patterns.

Why is it valuable to audit your working time? We know what eats up our time, right? Again, you are most probably wrong. Remember those cognitive biases and the 'Dunning-Kruger effect' we all suffer from? They don't stop with the list I had previously recounted. We are also a poor judge of the time we possess and how long it *really* takes to complete our working tasks.

Perhaps we are spending too much time devising lesson resources, or our lesson plans are consuming our every waking moment? If we lack the requisite balance, we need to reconfigure our use of time.

There is another law: 'Hofstadter's law'. This one states that work always takes longer than expected. It is a good rule of thumb. We could simplify it down to the *planning fallacy.* You think your lesson plans can be done in fifteen minutes, but they take twice as long. You go online for a simple definition or image and quickly lose an hour to the procrastination fairies searching for insignificant images down the bottom of the Google garden.

It is not only the temptation of the black hole of the Internet, or a chat (dare I say with no purpose except the sheer pleasure of chatting with our teacher friends), that is the main thief of our time and productivity. It is our inability to get organised and manage our time.

Where do I start? Make a list

I have read hundreds of thousands of words about to-do lists. In short, there are lots of ways of going about it, though many a guru will stake their claim to the most effective method.

First, let me assure you, I am no guru, and that the simple act of making a list will not defy the urge to procrastinate. It will not make you a more confident teacher, but it may give you a crucial start on both counts. Simply the act of writing a list helps you see the shape of your school day emerge into something like a plan.

How often are you too busy to make this list? Be honest. It is the waves of seemingly urgent work that is killing our productivity, which in turn deflates our confidence, meaning we are unable to get things done.

One bona fide productivity guru is Dave Allen. He has devised the simplest guide for your working to-do list with his *4 Ds of productivity*:

Do – Delegate – Defer – Drop

Here, Allen is dealing with the crucial aspect of prioritisation. We cannot do it all (we may not be able to do the half of it sometimes). With difficulty, we are managing our way through the seeming chaos of the day as best we can. Some jobs need to be dropped; some inessential emails have to wait.

We must remember that we have crucial work to do, but that we must also consider what we will *not* do. You may commit to *not* creating a raft of time-consuming resources and instead you will find something ready-made (as imperfect as it may be), thereby conserving energy and time to allocate elsewhere on your to-do list.

We are all instinctively biased towards action. As an English teacher, I make the annual plea to my students to plan in exams. The truth is that under pressure, students forsake planning and hurry into writing. We can fall into the same trap. We rush headlong into work and get started on the first job that is clouding our emotions. We lurch from job to job and we do not prioritise.

School leaders can often be to blame for adding tasks to the teacher workload, without ever taking things away. Consider a new curriculum initiative. It may look and sound great to implement a new model of online assessment, but if we challenge and ask what assessment are we removing to compensate for this new mode of working, then we may go some way to making the teacher workload healthier.

Lao Tzu, a Chinese sage, put it best:

> In pursuit of knowledge, every day something is acquired; in pursuit of wisdom, every day something is dropped.[2]

Consider what you can drop off your to-do list. School leaders would be well advised to do the same.

My rule of thumb is simple. Forget your tablet and phone organisers. If you cannot fit your to-do list for the day on a humble Post-it® note then you are not likely to complete your hoped for list. Try it: grab a Post-it® note and get listing. You won't be able to write much, which of course is the point. Completing the smaller, more realistic list, also has the added bonus of giving you the confidence boost of getting through your work.

So, grab your stack of Post-it® notes. Take your school day ahead. You have your fixed time: your lessons and your meetings. Start there. *What tasks relate to each fixed event? Have you planned your lesson? Are resources at hand? Have you read the documents required for your meeting? Are you adequately prepared for any contributions you will make?*

When you have listed the essential tasks related to your fixed time you are ready to prioritise. *What fluid tasks are at hand? How long do you have to complete said tasks?*

A pragmatic approach is to deal with tasks chronologically. If student reports aren't due for a fortnight, then deferring that task is a likely result; yet, sometimes, getting ahead of the curve can save you pain in the future. *Does writing your reports now, perhaps in small, manageable batches, mean that come the report deadline you can concentrate on marking the assessment that is due on the same day?* Perhaps you can manage the reports in more tolerable batches (essential in the fight against the raging crow of procrastination) – say five reports a day.

This is an example of the 'small daily task' that Trollope heralds as defeating Hercules. It just takes some planning and organisation, with no little willpower. Consider it your new healthy 'five-a-day' work routine.

Balance the urgent tasks with your strategic forward planning. Make that planning sacrosanct in the regular creases of your working week. Perhaps it is ten minutes at the start of the day on Monday, and then it's Wednesday and Friday first thing too. To be strategic we must commit time to planning and to our to-do lists, despite the incessant slings and arrows of urgent demands.

The fatal error of most procrastinators is they don't devote enough time to planning their time.

I have often found myself in awe of teachers who appeared to effortlessly juggle their job list. I was flailing about with scraps of paper, bashing from class to class like a fairground dodgem ride. When you are so mired in the stresses and strains of the day, you have scant mental energy to commit to strategic forward planning.

I am now a full convert to the power of making strategic checklists. I see so many confident teacher experts using this method that to do anything other appears foolish. I run a master to-do list (I have an app for that), and then a daily 'Post-it® note to-do list', ensuring I prioritise and knock them off and don't overestimate what I can do in the short span of a day.

My check listing extends to my management of email. My endless torrent of emails is now always organised into folders and subfolders. I set aside time in the summer to set up the folders and keep this up weekly. Strategy is all.

Importantly, popping emails away in folders and seeing an ordered inbox gives us a feeling of control, which is often essential for our psychological well-being, even when we may not have completed the job itself. We know such a *locus of control* – the feeling of being in control – has a beneficial impact upon our confidence.

If I have a large task then I create a 'project', with an attendant email folder, whereat the greater goal is broken down into its component tasks. For example, if I am teaching a new syllabus, then I need to create a list of smaller tasks: ordering copies of the specification from the exam board; doing some wider reading on the Internet; planning new lesson sequences; arranging for co-planning sessions with my colleagues. Each task can be allocated in a sequence, each with an estimated time of completion (remembering that we are poor at predicting our own work timings, so erring on the pessimistic side).

In his *Checklist Manifesto*, Atul Gawande, an expert surgeon and checklist champion, argues persuasively that using checklists doesn't make you some unthinking robot. Instead, it frees you up to respond more flexibly to the dizzying complexity of the school day.

Managing such complexity can prove stressful, but a good checklist can mitigate this anxiety. Harry Fletcher-Wood was so influenced by his experience as a teacher using checklists that he went and wrote a book about it: 'What I only came to appreciate much later was the calming effect they can have as well. I learned to trust the checklists I wrote: to go through each item, reassure myself I'd done it, and then relax.'

Though not a quick fix for all our workload ills, Fletcher-Wood describes the positive psychological impact a checklist can have: 'Preparing for a stressful situation, I use checklists both to make sure I have done everything I should do in advance, and to help me feel in control of what's coming. Checklist done, I have completed everything I am smart enough to have thought of in advance – and will just have to trust to luck for anything else.'

Checklists, once they become an automatic habit, can help free us from the stress of missing small but important details in our working day. Yes – checklists cannot capture every detail of our teaching week, but they can give coherence to most of what we do. They are valuable tools for the busy teacher.

Are you a morning person?

Hopefully, I have convinced you of the value of making daily 'Post-it® to-do lists', alongside more detailed project checklists. Though not necessarily pleasurable, both are essential to managing your time confidently. With that act now in mind, when should you compose your to-do list?

Of course, we can all revel in our unique foibles, but sometimes we need to defer to the best evidence about what works. The best time to write your to-do list is very likely first thing in the morning. Not convinced? A research study of Israeli judges may persuade you otherwise.

Judges, those bastions of rational thought, were found to make some worryingly flawed judgements. After analysing over a thousand parole board hearings, it became obvious that the likelihood of your being paroled rested not simply on the facts, but based on the time of day that the hearing took place.

Israeli judges, just like teachers, suffer from 'decision fatigue'. Those prisoners who appeared in the morning were given parole 70 per cent of the time, compared to a paltry 10 per cent of those judged late in the day.[3] This study helps support the notion that our willpower and our judgement can be hampered by fatigue.

Tired and no doubt hungry, the judges reverted to the safer option of denying parole. To consider that our decisions may be compromised by the absence of a sandwich should give us pause.

We see it in our students' behaviour in the afternoon. We feel it ourselves, when sparked into conflict by an equally tired and hungry student. We are all too human after all. Being conscious of the time of day, our diet and our energy levels, goes some way in helping us better manage our productivity.

Why doesn't Barack Obama choose his own suits and why does that matter to humble teachers? Or why did Steve Jobs, Apple guru, become synonymous with a black turtleneck sweater? Why does Mark Zuckerberg, Facebook CEO, wear grey T-shirts over and over? It isn't for the want of a few dollars to bolster their wardrobe – it was a conscious decision to reduce their decision fatigue first thing in the morning.

Just like the Israeli judges, these leaders were decision-makers and every decision they could avoid saved some crucial mental energy. We need to make important decisions while our mind is at our peak. We may not be running a national superpower or a corporate giant, but don't underestimate the importance of the huge number of decisions we undertake each day.

This all leads to writing that to-do list first thing in the morning. A simple ten minutes prioritising what we need to do with our fluid time that day – thinking carefully through the potential pitfalls and deciding on what to *do*, *delegate*, *defer* or *drop* – goes a long way.

It can prove remarkable how much clarity and confidence can be gained by such a short investment of time. As the time of day research proves, we are all morning people of sorts. As teachers, it becomes a necessity that we fight the urge to be relentlessly busy so that we can make plans.

Despite our conditioning as hard-working teachers, we are still weighed down by our evolutionary past. In our distant past we only needed to maintain our concentration for a short span of minutes to hunt and such. Taking short breaks throughout the day is still a necessity if we are to preserve our willpower and perform confidently and competently.

There is a deep-rooted problem here. Our western culture promotes the notion that we can only be effective when we are relentlessly busy. Persistent hard work doesn't factor in stopping to rest and take stock. The evidence proves that breaks actually enhance our overall effectiveness. Even a short break can recharge our minds ready to once again teach confidently. Simply the act of letting our mind wander can prove restful in the face of our 'always working' culture.

Just remember that it is essential to avoid the devilish influence of technology so that you can properly mentally recharge. There is a reason why Facebook use peaks at 11am and 3pm on weekdays (surveyed, ironically, by a media management company named Virtue). It is an indication of the modern *cyber-loafing* phenomenon.

The compulsion to fill our free time with the addictive power of the Web and social media is felt less in the busy environment of the school, but this compulsion is unhealthy and can damage our professional confidence. So, how can we better manage this issue with some confident control?

Technology – a tool for productivity or procrastination?

Picture the familiar scenario. You arrive at work feeling spritely and surprisingly alert for a Monday morning. Spring freshness has filled the air and spurred you forth into school. You grab a drink and chat casually about a fun-filled weekend. You are just about to commit to your Post-it® note to-do list.

Before you finish your conversation you unthinkingly log into the school computer. The familiar raft of emails is stuffing your inbox to the rafters. One email stands out amidst the others. The boss wants to quickly chat about an issue with a parent, but she cannot see you until lunchtime.

What happens next?

The familiar signs of anxiety are alive in your every move. Each task is tainted by your fear and loathing of the prospect of lunchtime and what may come. Your willpower drains away and your teaching suffers. We are all subject to these damaging emotions, and they blot our thinking and can ruin our time management.

Those of us old enough to remember being given endless paper notes through the school day may recognise the obvious benefits of email communication, but we should approach the keyboard with much forethought.

That small shot of endorphin as we open the message can turn us into email-o-holics. We can feel a false sense of productivity. The octopus-like reach of email into every facet of our lives can become pervasive. One AOL survey showed that 59 per cent of people check their emails on the toilet![4]

My personal experience has proven one thing for me: responding to email guarantees you one thing...*more emails*. CCing creates problems too. We think putting others 'in the loop' could save us some vital time, but in many cases it simply compels them to reply too – exponentially growing yet more emails.

Yes – there are tricks to guard against being emailed at all hours, such as clever settings to slightly reduce our email count, but ultimately the impact of email needs to be thought about deeply at a school level. Our working effectively depends on it.

Email can prove a destructive force for our to-do list. We need to make emailing a discrete item on our list, not something we do at each and every moment of the day. Make a judgement about each email you receive: is the topic too complex and therefore requiring face-to-face communication? If so, simple: don't reply.

Too often, we get locked into an endless email chain to compensate for such complexity. Is the topic personal or emotive? If so, avoid the chain and find a time to speak in person. It may lose a short time in travel, but our well-being, and that of our colleagues, may be at stake.

If an email is more than a week old, place it in an 'old emails' subfolder. It is remarkable how refreshing a near empty inbox can prove. It is an equally liberating realisation that the vast majority of emails are inessential and can be soon deleted. Give each email a fortnight. If you haven't replied in that time it will never prove urgent enough to take up your time.

Press delete.

Are you wholly reliant on mobile technology? Does your work mean that you are 'always on'? Think carefully about having a technological blackout at specific times, particularly in your evening, to help divide the lines between your work and play more clearly. Your willpower may well depend upon it.

Is email all bad? Of course, there are uses and effective methods of reducing your workload and improving your organisation with technology. I have a very useful electronic calendar and a task management app like many teachers. It is all about intelligent usage, which overrides the urge to procrastinate and tangle us in email chains. Indeed, there are now lots of applications to help us block our favourite websites, stick to our timed tasks and tie us down to our essential jobs.

A good example is using technology to improve the effectiveness of a meeting. Sending or receiving prior reading electronically, rather than wasting fifteen minutes of the actual meeting time reading, can often prove a boon to the quality and impact of the meeting itself. I am no Luddite – but we should be wary of seeing technology as a time-saving panacea.

Monotonous meetings and what to do about them

Every teacher of every stripe spends at least some of his or her working week in meetings. Given that they are a staple of our fixed time, we should aim to make them as productive as possible. You may not be the school leader who has convened the meeting, but you can still influence the meeting regardless of your status (if you show a little confidence).

One classic error is pursuing an absurdly long meeting – exhausting the participants and achieving little. Puncture this by citing the research which proves that our judgement after an hour of any meeting is seriously impaired. Not only is the meeting tiring, it could prove counterproductive.

Help by sharing some golden rules of effective meetings:

- Have a meeting agenda.
- Stick to the agenda.
- Stick to the time parameters of the meeting outlined on the agenda.
- Have clear roles and responsibilities for the meeting – put them on the agenda.
- Any item that does not involve at least 80 per cent of the people attending should not be on the agenda.
- Consider carefully who exactly needs to attend the meeting. Yes – regular meetings can increase the unity of a group of teachers, but if it consumes too much time for little benefit then the results will prove

counterproductive. Remember the 'Rule of 7': for every teacher in the meeting beyond this number, the likelihood of making a good, relatively speedy decision drops.

- If something can be read or researched before the meeting, which would save valuable time to discuss and move the meeting on, then organise to have teachers read it beforehand.

You may not be leading the meeting, but ask for the agenda, clear timings and meeting roles etc. Helping 'manage' the meeting leader, from near or far, will be in the best interests of everybody involved.

Perfectionism – the enemy of productivity

Sometimes we face simple truths that make our lives easier, reduce our stress and increase our happiness. Here is one such truth: *work is better done than perfect.*

The pursuit of perfection is too often underpinned by a lack of personal confidence. We may feel anxiety about how our colleagues will perceive us if we don't produce a flawless lesson plan, or we may worry that students will not respect us if we do not give them detailed personal feedback on each piece of work they do.

We must not be too hard on ourselves. We are busy professionals, with lives, families and recognisably sizeable workloads.

Of course, it is best not to make mistakes – we all feel that – but does your fear of mistakes mean you draft emails to colleagues over and over before you press send? Do you spend an hour preparing a single lesson plan or resource? Do you spend more time preparing for a meeting than you will actually spend being in the meeting? If the answer is yes, then you may need to recognise that your perfectionist streak is making you unproductive.

I take great pride in my teaching and my writing. Both take a significant amount of my time. And yet it wasn't until I gained the confidence to make mistakes – sending emails out with a singular check, rather than agonising over every word multiple times – that I started to find I could better meet my priorities. I gained the confidence in my experience to plan lessons quickly, consciously leaving gaps in my plans. In reality, those gaps would prove a boon: I could adapt and be flexible to what my students needed without feeling chained to a detailed lesson plan.

School leaders can help. There needs to be a school culture which recognises that failure and making mistakes is normal and not to be feared. There needs to be a school culture that doesn't encourage a slavish adherence to unnecessary paperwork, such as never-ending lesson plan templates.

A good antidote to perfectionism is the confident recognition that we can only be the best version of ourselves, rather than comparing ourselves to others, or to unrealistically high standards.

Daily rituals and routines

Meetings usually occur at the end of the school day. After an energy and willpower sapping marathon, we are expected to be creative, combative, thorough, insightful and more. Unsurprisingly, we usually aren't.

A bad meeting, sparked by shortened fuses and generating little more than extra work, can bleed into the rest of our evening. Our day no longer feels our own. The seeming endlessness of our teacher workload is compounded by our inability to leave work at work. In the distant past, there were clearer thresholds at the ends of the working day. In our modern jobs, the pervasive presence of technology means that we are never far away from work infiltrating our every waking thought and tiring us out.

Routines and habits can help us preserve our precious mental energy. Rituals at the end of the day, in particular, can be crucial in sending ourselves the important signal to let go of the working day.

Perhaps you clear your desk, check through your Post-it® note to-do list, or even play your favourite song. This ritual, allied with your determination to have some time to yourself, could be coupled with you turning off your emails and your phone, or making other obvious work-stopping actions. First, we must convince ourselves that these breaks are not just important for our sanity, but for our working creativity and productivity.

Ultimately, we aren't in control of many aspects of our working day, but we must control what we can, when we can. Even these small decisions we implement in our working day can marginally enhance our self-confidence and our sense of control. Being better organised can preserve your energy levels, which every teacher knows is crucial if they are to not just cope, but to thrive with confidence.

We can start tomorrow, with some small and less than Herculean tasks.

It is a little like learning to play the saxophone. How would you plan to learn? Would you cram all your sessions into one single evening, or would you break up your practice into short, more regular sessions? Our workload is no different. Planning to ensure this can happen is the key.

As suggested earlier in the chapter, if faced with the daunting task of fifty essays to mark, or reports to write, then start with a daily 'five-a-day'. Even better, aim to calendar your written feedback so that each of your classes complete their assessments at a slightly different time, so that you can schedule these smaller-scale tasks more often. It is apocryphal, but making a start is the best defence against procrastination. If you have failed to plan and prioritise, you may not have enough days left to do your daily five-a-day.

As teachers, we have a core purpose to drive us forward. We have children in our care who depend upon us, along with trusted colleagues too. This pull typically proves enough to persevere in doing that trickiest of things: developing good working habits.

IN SHORT...

- Joining a gym spikes in January, but we know that 92 per cent of New Year's resolutions fail.[5] Four out of five gym memberships go unused. These facts are testimony to our finite willpower and the difficulty in building sustained habit changes. We need to plan with these natural flaws in mind.
- Remember, we underestimate how long tasks will take, and we overestimate our capacity to stick to our habits. Adjust your working habits to address these flaws.
- Our expectation that we can quickly and easily become more productive teachers is a misnomer. Like developing self-confidence, becoming more productive is a process of arduous effort that requires planning, commitment and reflection.
- We must remember that, counter-intuitively, inaction is sometimes the best form of action.
- Perfectionism is the enemy of productivity: do it, try it and share it. If it doesn't work, learn from it and try it again. Fail better.

- We should devise checklists and use effective personal organisers, but we should also be wary of technology proving a hindrance to our productivity.
- Finally, if we prepare, plan and prioritise our teaching day, whilst strategically planning our weeks and terms, then we better provide ourselves with the conditions for confident productivity.

Notes

1 Trollope, A. (2008), *An Autobiography and Other Writings*. Oxford: Oxford University Press.

2 Tzu, L., cited in Muller, W. (1999), *Sabbath: Restoring the Sacred Rhythm of Rest*, p 134. New York: Bantam.

3 Danziger, S., Levav, J. and Avnaim-Pesso, L. (2011), 'Extraneous factors in judicial decisions', *PNAS* 108 (17).

4 AOL. 'The 2010 AOL Email Survey' [Online]. Available at: http://cdn.webmail.aol.com/survey/aol/en-us/ (Accessed: 10 November 2014).

5 Statistic Brain (2015), 'New year's resolution statistics'. [Online]. Available at: www.statisticbrain.com/new-years-resolution-statistics/ (Accessed: 24 January 2015).

Section 2
Our confident body

6 A healthy body and mind

A healthy mind is often twinned with a healthy body. This age-old saying, attributed to the Greek philosopher, Thales, has been at the beating heart of education in the Western world since its known inception:

Who is happy? The person who has a healthy body, a resourceful mind and a docile nature.

The arts and physical education were at the very core of a Greek liberal education and our physical life was explicitly seen as enriching our intellectual capacity.

In more recent centuries, the mind has been raised on a symbolic pedestal above the body, not just a literal one. In schools, this implicit hierarchy, relegating everything below the neck, is alive and well in most of that we do. Physical education, for example, is a poor sibling to the heavyweights of the subject hierarchy: mathematics, the sciences and more.

It is also true of much of our teacher training and development. The uniquely physical act of teaching is too often relegated from discussion, thereby neglecting a fundamental aspect of our craft. A common, if rather hackneyed, analogy for a teacher is that of an actor performing on the classroom stage each day. The energy stealing implication of this day-in-day-out routine reaches somewhere near the truth. Yet, curiously, our teacher training marginalises the importance of non-verbal communication. The whole act is shunted off stage.

There is usually a small dose of voice training, perhaps early on, with a behaviour management session or two that integrates some physical practice and movement, but non-verbal communication takes a distant back seat to theory and pedagogy. How can we ignore such a crucial component of our craft? How many marginal opportunities for improvement do we miss?

We must make this implicit knowledge of the body explicit. We know that expert teachers move and communicate in subtle but, quite literally, telling ways. By first understanding the nuances of non-verbal communication, we can then enact a better grasp of the physical act of teaching. The rewards are once more improved competence and increased confidence.

Our world is saturated by visual images of the physical body. How we see people can fundamentally shift what we think about what they say, and teachers are no different. Famously, in 1960, presidential hopeful, John F Kennedy, squared off against Richard Nixon in the first ever televised presidential debate. An audience of 76 million watched as a confident and calm young Irish senator debated against an apparently sickly and nervous vice president. It is said that radio listeners voted Nixon the winner, but the television audience voted overwhelmingly for the smiling and very visible new star of American politics.

Now, happily, teachers aren't forced to perform in front of an eager audience of millions, but the lesson is obvious: how we present ourselves physically – how we *perform* – matters.

Right or wrong, people better trust what we say when they perceive we are confident, and they more naturally defer to a confident speaker. For those of us who have watched a teacher wilt under the lights like Nixon, before seeing the students lose confidence in their ability, will know that this matters deeply for all teachers.

People, both adults and children, often mistake overt shows of physical confidence with competence. Though I do not recommend faking competence as a strategy, we should ensure that we harness this shortcut in human thinking.

I like to think of it as the *graceful swan effect*. If we give the impression in our physical actions that we are in complete control, that we are assured and confident, then people will invariably believe it. This is just as important for the new teacher masking their terror in the classroom, to the head teacher speaking with power to her teaching staff.

First, think of those role model experts you have been taught by, or you have observed teaching. If you consider deeply, you can likely paint a picture of their mannerisms, their verbal fluency, the seemingly effortless control of their classroom space. If I think deeply about my time in school, I can even recall the unique nuances of gesture and speech of my favourite teachers. The classroom was all theirs. Somehow, whether they were tiny or slight in stature, quiet or humble in their manner, they were in complete physical command of the classroom.

A healthy body and mind

Our students instinctively *feel* the importance of our body language, often unconsciously, and it is essential in eliciting trust and creating the conditions for our students to be receptive to learning.

Blink and you'll miss it

In human nature, but especially in the role of teaching, we make momentary judgements based on sight and the smallest of physical actions. Malcolm Gladwell's hugely successful book, *Blink: The Power of Thinking Without Thinking*, captures the notion that most of our decisions are made instantaneously.

If I consider the actions of many of my students, I can testify to the power of instinctive, sometimes irrational, responses. We like to think our practice as teachers is in the iron grip of our rational control, only it isn't. Our own mental biases, psychological flaws and physical limitations beset us. The best we can do is better recognise these personal foibles, and in understanding them, deal with them more confidently. It is imperative we do so because our physical confidence matters if we are to become teacher experts.

Consider the smallest action of simply smiling. Now, imagine your boss smiling at you.

Perhaps it shouldn't, but whether we like it or not, such a small event lingers long in the mind and can have a disproportionate emotional impact upon us. The oft-given advice to new teachers to 'not smile before Christmas' appears rather foolish in light of such evidence (more on that later).

Consider other tiny details of physical communication. There is a great deal of research to support the power of snap judgements: from trustworthiness judged from a momentary facial expression, to people who give eye contact being considered more intelligent, whereas those lacking eye contact are deemed as less intelligent. Even simply speaking quickly can be wrongly associated with anxiety.

In the cold light of print, these judgements seem irrational and a little absurd, but they remind us that teaching and learning is bound up in a physical and social act. Relationships matter. How we physically relate to students, and our teaching colleagues, leaves an indelible impression.

Teaching amidst the crowd

Our bodies are acutely attuned to our lives as teachers. How many times have you crept to the end of term, only to fall ill with tiredness and stress? Our mental lives as teachers are inextricably bound to our physical selves.

The physical stress of teaching pushes us to the edge of our natural capacity. We were only ever designed to work in small groups or tribes. Our hunter-gatherer instincts would balk at the mass of humanity spilling around the school dining hall. The sheer number of human physical relationships is exhausting.

The part of the brain that deals with human relations, the neocortex, has a primal basis, reaching back to our heritage as primates. In short, there are only so many fellow apes we can pick fleas from, or to put it in modern terms, there are only so many people in our working day we can sustain relationships with. For the introvert teacher, the effort can prove even tougher.

Robin Dunbar, a British anthropologist, has staked his name in history with *Dunbar's number*: the theory that one hundred and fifty is the limit for human relationships for any one person. Luckily, Dunbar's number, and our brains, allow for just enough resources to deal with a bunch of young primates assailing us four or five times each day.

That isn't to say that it is natural to relate to so many people in a given day. With the accumulated needs and whims of our student brethren, it is no surprise that our willpower is sometimes shot and our capacity to function is dimmed. Many teachers will know the guilt that attends to returning home to our own family, only to be exhausted by people and wanting only peace and quiet.

The physical toll of teaching

Back in the day, this day being in 400 BC, Hippocrates suggested that going for walks would help cure many of our ills and refresh our minds. Take a look at this list: William Wordsworth, Charles Darwin, Jane Austen, Charles Dickens and Steve Jobs. The connection? Each one of these luminaries walked daily to generate ideas and they perambulated through the history books and into our common consciousness.

We all want to stave off heart disease, depression, high blood pressure and their ilk. Walking, with the aerobic exercise it generates, can, like sleeping, help keep our precious brain and our body in good working order.

Research has shown that walking can also charge up the hippocampus, the region of the brain involved in learning and our verbal memory. We cannot wander our way to genius, but we can clear our minds and boost ourselves for a busy working day.

Teachers hunched over their computers at lunchtime, getting lost in a tangle of data and student marking, won't be anywhere near as refreshed as the teacher who has had a good lunch and perhaps even a little meander around school.

Going for a country walk like Darwin may not be very practical when you are teaching a full timetable in a day, but even a conscious focus on taking a wander, such as committing to speaking to someone at another spot in the school, rather than writing another email, can prove beneficial.

Now, you may be forgiven for thinking that there have been many lessons where you would have gladly walked out of and onto a path less travelled. Instead, we are metaphorically tied to the teacher desk. But when did you last choose to go for a lunchtime walk? Making time for such small habits can make a difference.

Once more, in our attempt to be productive, chasing the modern disease of 'busyness', we leave a proper lunch in an attempt to catch up with our many jobs. This not only compromises our health, it can also make us less creative and less productive, whilst leaving us susceptible to making poor decisions in the classroom and beyond.

Of course, we often speak about how the nutrition of our students can equally impact upon their behaviour.[1] Yet, seldom do we talk in any depth about how we eat during the day, the breaks we take, or our sleep regime. Our body is often treated as little more than transport for our brain. We should change this paradigm for our personal benefit and for our professional confidence.

Yes, we can say 'I think, therefore I am', but we need to eat and sleep well so that we can think with clarity and teach with confidence.

Relationships, relationships, relationships

A few years ago, some past students spoke to me about our fondly remembered English class. I enjoyed teaching them and thankfully the feeling appeared to be mutual. One comment in passing did surprise me though. They relayed how they would judge my mood when I walked in the room, or in the first moments when they walked into the room.

It turned out, unbeknownst to me, that I was both moody and sometimes plain grumpy. When I was happy, they would relax and enjoy the lessons a great deal more. Now, whether they learnt any more or less when I was in a sour mood is debatable, but my surprise that I was so beholden to my moods, and so physically transparent, made me think deeply about my practice.

Still a relatively new teacher then, I was tired and stressed, scaling heights of happiness (mixed with relief) and then crashing back to earth, lesson by lesson. Now, with more confidence and competence, my mood is more even and my tiredness proves less pronounced than before. Students can better trust my mood and, in all likelihood, the quality of my teaching. Perhaps that is what Thales meant by a happy, confident and 'docile nature'.

We are social and emotional beings. Social connectedness is a basic need, just like food and shelter. Teaching and learning is little different. Our students are acutely attuned to our emotions. In the age of the spreadsheet, we should be mindful that teaching will always be a deeply personal act of communication – one defined by trust and care. Teachers are motivated by their emotions and the emotional geography of teaching is in part physical rather than solely intellectual.

When we are confident and happy we are open to giving a little of ourselves. Instances like this occur daily: an explanation is illuminated by one of our personal stories, or we more easily laugh and convey our ease. Students feed off those conditions and trust grows. This trust is an essential prerequisite for listening, taking risks, fostering ideas and for successful learning.

By all means, communicate a rich passion for your subject, that will go a long way to encouraging students to immerse themselves in the pleasures and challenges of learning, but it won't prove enough alone. You will have to be equally passionate about developing relationships and communicating with young people.

Our job as a teacher is both thinking and physical, mind and body, professional and personal.

> ## IN SHORT...
>
> - All teachers, whether they are developing their craft, being trained, or training others, should be mindful that teaching is always a physical act and that we should devote due care and attention to our physical communication.
> - Even the smallest acts of our physical communication matter, from a momentary smile to the raising of a hand to becalm a debate. Blink and you'll miss them, but don't underestimate their enduring impact.
> - Remember the 'graceful swan effect'. Most teachers are metaphorically kicking like mad through much of the school week, but those who hide it best are often seen as the most confident amongst us, and this matters.
> - It was true of Thales' ancient Greece as it is now: the best role model for our students is always a healthy and happy teacher.

Note

1 Gesch, B. (2014), 'Adolescence: Does good nutrition = good behaviour?' University of Oxford, UK. [Online]. Available at: http://nah.sagepub.com/content/22/1/55.abstract (Accessed: 20 February 2015).

7 Combatting stress

Few teachers have escaped the chastening experience of a lesson gone awry – that lesson when your students inexplicably descend into a subtle madness. Every attempt at focus and control feels like a fool's errand, with your best-laid plans left in tatters by your hormone-fuelled students.

For a short time, the pen-smeared whiteboard dissolves away to present something like a cloud-filled, dry savannah. The hunt is on. The pack circles; the teacher-hunter betrays their lack of sureness.

We are exposed. Our façade of control teeters dangerously. The breath quickens. Blood pounds against the walls of our strained blood vessels. Even momentarily, our response becomes primal. Our bodies have been primed for this very scenario: fight or flight.

It is moments like these that define our professional confidence. These are moments of high stress. How do we conquer them? How do we best prepare for them happening? How do we respond to failure when it occurs? How do we best read and manage our emotions?

How do we stay resilient in these trying circumstances? Answering this question will go a long way to developing our confidence.

A stressful vocation

First, it is important to define what I mean by stress in this chapter. There is a significant difference between the chronic stress that requires clinical help and the daily stresses that beset our busy lives as teachers.

Where the boundary between manageable and chronic stress resides is a difficult question to answer. Too many small, seemingly manageable stresses and we can suffer from hypertension. Get stressed too often and our blood flow damages our blood vessels, kills neurons in our brain and damages our judgement. Crucially, our daily stresses can be better managed with effective strategies we can deploy and with well-timed support.

Our brains were designed to deal with stress, indeed to use stress, but only in short bursts. When you have no sense of control over your job as a teacher, with the pressures and expectations of doing a good job for your students, your family and yourself, the constant negative stress can be debilitating. Like low-level chatter in a classroom, it can rise to a persistent clamour.

Stress, like low self-confidence, has been pathologised, with a freight-train industry of drugs, expertise and coping strategies to attend it. It is seemingly the scourge of the modern workplace: in a UK government study, between October 2011 and January 2013, 35 per cent of sickness notes accounting for work absence were given for 'mild to moderate mental health disorders'.[1]

It isn't just weak, failing, or lazy teachers who suffer from negative stress, as is sometimes the ill-considered caricature. High-performing teachers are pushed to the edge of their limits too. The latest government-commissioned survey in the United Kingdom has teachers working in excess of fifty hours a week.[2] These are the very conditions where negative stress can thrive and spread like a virus.

Stress damages your brain, hampering your *executive function* – effectively your ability to manage your decisions and your self-control – so crucial to dealing with a mass of potentially truculent teenagers. It can also damage our memory. Stress heightens our emotional memory and therefore our failures that trigger our stresses loom larger in our mind. It is a vicious psychological circle and all too familiar for the large number of teachers who leave the profession early.

We too easily think in black-and-white terms when stressed. If a lesson is imperfect, we jump on those small mistakes. Our tendency to fixate on failure can make us foresee a catastrophe in each and every event, seeking out the worst-case scenario in every situation to our detriment. This damaging response can prove emotionally contagious in a school department or faculty.

It is hard to foster self-confidence when our thinking is so clouded by such debilitating stress. We can miss the many small wins and it can lead to a spiral toward burnout[3] for some. The problem is real, but the solutions are often obscured for busy teachers.

Recognising the signs of stress

For too many teachers, negative stress is commonplace in our working lives – so much so that it becomes invisible to us. The common signs of stress will be familiar to teachers everywhere. Some of the signs of negative stress include:

- Problems related to lack of sleep
- Excessive tiredness throughout the day
- Problems related to appetite: from excessive 'comfort eating' to under-eating
- Prone to being emotionally erratic
- Prone to indecision and overreaction
- Lacking in motivation and self-confidence
- An inability to concentrate and memory issues
- Aches and pains, headaches, diarrhoea or constipation, loss of libido, chest pain and rapid heartbeat

We have all faced these stress factors at one time or another, but when they are experienced cumulatively they can lead to professional burnout. We need to recognise our negative stresses, monitoring our stress levels, and taking action when required.

There are two helpful acronyms that can help us better recognise our negative stress levels and those of our colleagues. The first is **HALT**, which provides a useful reminder for a sequence of checks:

> **H** – Check you are not too Hungry
> **A** – Check you are not too Angry
> **L** – Check you are not too Lonely
> **T** – Check you are not too Tired

The second useful acronym is **IMSAFE**, which is a quick catalogue of issues related to stress:

> **I** – Illness
> **M** – Medication
> **S** – Stress
> **A** – Alcohol
> **F** – Fatigue
> **E** – Emotion

Each of the issues above can prove subtle indicators of everyday stress, to warning signs of something more serious. We are all prone to running the gamut of emotions, but being more clearly erratic emotionally can be a signal for excessive stress. Similarly, becoming reliant on alcohol to manage the working day is something very different to having a glass of wine as an accompaniment to an evening meal.

One way to track our personal stresses is to keep a diary over the course of a fortnight or so, making a note of aspects like where and when we were stressed, alongside how we felt, before rating the degree of stress on a simple scale. It works just like the time audit suggested in Chapter 5. It is about becoming mindful of our emotional and physical reactions on typical working days. By tracking our stress levels and being more mindful of our emotional well-being, we can begin to pin down what triggers our stresses and how we respond under pressure.

We can balance a focus on our 'daily hassles' with an equivalent focus on our 'daily uplifts'.[4] Yes – having to input data for multiple classes can prove maddening, but it can be quickly alleviated by a laugh-laden chat with a friend. Consider stress here like a set of scales. Our stresses can build up, but we can keep them in balance by finding ways to lift our mood. This will take some planning, but the effort should prove worthwhile.

There is no quick fix and we will all respond differently to the circumstances of negative work stress. For many teachers, self-help strategies won't be nearly enough and there will be occasions when our negative stress levels are such that we require medical support and you will need to contact your doctor. For some, leaving the profession, what I would consider a last resort, is the only answer and is to be respected and not demeaned.

Self-help can go so far, but our job as a teacher, thankfully, is founded on our relationships with our colleagues and our students, so being vigilant of negative stress in those around us becomes a crucial responsibility for us all. There is no more important task we can undertake than take care of our colleagues, and students, looking out for them and helping them recognise when they are negatively stressed and supporting them to better deal with their difficulties.

Schools leaders play a central role in helping teachers manage their negative stress. Leaders can apply simple principles for every action they undertake and each decision they implement. They can ask the questions: if we are to implement this change, what will we drop? If we are to add this task for teachers, what task will we take away? What support factors need to be in place for our teachers to flourish?

School leaders must make a conscious effort to ensure teachers feel valued and that they have an authentic voice in the decision-making process. A great deal of negative stress can emerge from teachers feeling like they are not trusted – or that there is too little confidence in them. In these circumstances, it is easy to feel helpless and to ascribe failures to our rubbish school, rather than something we can change.

In short, the point here is obvious: if school leaders were to undertake a concerted effort to improve the well-being of teachers, then the benefits can prove significant for teachers and schools. We need a culture in which negative stress is talked about and not stigmatised. Crucially, we need to understand stress and better interpret its purpose and usefulness.

Good stress

The picture of teacher stress I have painted is a bleak one so far, but some balance is required.

Mention the word 'stress' in a crowded school staffroom and the word is likely to spark a litany of complaints. The boss, fellow teachers, an uproarious student – everyone is fair game when the stressed teacher unloads their canon. Perhaps we are part of the problem. Indeed, our very perception of stress can prove, well...plain stressful!

Research has found that if we perceive that the stress we are feeling will negatively impact our health, then it can increase the risk of premature death by 43 per cent.[5] Put simply, if you think stress can be a positive, then you can actually reduce your chances of a stress-related death!

How much control we perceive we have over our all too human daily stresses really does matter a great deal.

One of Bandura's essential strategies for developing authentic confidence was how we better interpret our physical responses. This proves crucially important here. If we view the physical signs of stress more positively, then our body can believe us and respond in a healthier fashion. If we consider our heart pounding before we speak to a crowded exam hall, we tell ourselves that is our body working to get essential blood to our heart; if we are breathing fast, we tell ourselves that we are sending essential oxygen to our brain to think more clearly. We need to learn to see these stress indicators as positive and useful.

The endocrinologist Hans Selye even coined a word for it: *eustress* (the prefix 'eu' from the Greek meaning 'good'). It is very different from the types of chronic stress that can negatively affect our sleep, mood and our willpower at work. The right degree of stress makes us better at our job as a teacher. The etymology of the verb 'stress' – 'to emphasise' – is instructive.

We need this physical and emotional *emphasis* to help us prioritise what we do. Are you someone who works to deadlines? In which case, you are actively creating low-level *eustress* to work effectively. The night before a staff presentation are you struggling to sleep? Our brain is readying itself for what is a typically challenging experience in many respects. The sweaty palms and pounding heart are followed by a surge of excitement when you have conquered your fears.

As physical education teachers and sports coaches know well, a moderate amount of stress is required for peak performance. It is known as the 'Inverted U' of performance:

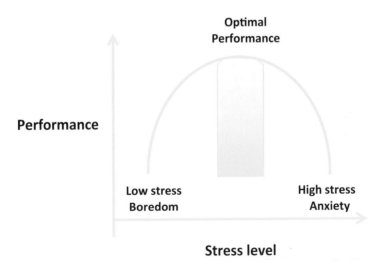

Figure 7.1

If we rethink the usefulness of stress as something more productive, and we couple that with good habits and support from our colleagues, then we will go a long way to mitigating our school-related daily stresses.

One other good attribute of stress is that it actually makes us more social. Oxytocin, a hormone released when we are stressed, primes us to relate better to others, boosting our capacity for empathy. In short, it gives us a shot of social confidence. Oxytocin is a stress response just like adrenaline, but it is our body actually telling us to speak with others about our stress. We know that emotions are contagious – but they can be for good or ill.

Negative stress can circulate the room and the school, but then so can optimism and hope. It takes collective effort and mutual support amongst our teaching colleagues, but that effort pays off in the most important of ways: our collective confidence can flourish.

This highlights that being supported by our colleagues, and supporting others, is absolutely crucial to our well-being, which in turn can increase or strangle our professional confidence. We can boost our resilience in the face of stress by having significant friendships, trusting our colleagues to share our problems and to give us support and guidance. Managing negative stress is about resilience and courage, but it is also about connecting with others and good team work. This is also why being, or becoming, a confident teacher can typically prove a collective experience.

Physical solutions to combatting stress

We know that how we perceive stress is important in helping us better combat its damaging effects. We also know about the power of productivity and organisation in heading off damaging levels of negative stress. So what else can we do when mired in a sea of troubles?

Here is my selection of just some of the simple ways we can seize control of our negative stresses, with an emphasis on our living, breathing and no doubt term-tired physical selves. They likely prove a reminder of common sense notions, but we can all do with a reminder every once in a while:

Straighten up

After a long day, our pulse rate and adrenaline has surged and settled over and over, and we are spent. The sheer weight of the day can fall upon our shoulders and we slump with tiredness. It is the same in every staffroom the world over.

The problem? Our natural response to the tiredness and stress of the school day: a hunched posture, or slumping in our chair, can worsen our mood and compound our stresses. The simple act of sitting upright in our chair can raise our mood in the face of stress.[6] Just being conscious of sitting up straight can make a small difference.

Eat, drink and be merry

Remember the Israeli judges and their mental energy being sapped before lunch and at the end of the day? A tired and hungry teacher simply cannot exercise all of their skills effectively either. And yet, teachers the world over are working through their lunchtimes, hunched over a computer, punching in data, finishing lesson plans and thereby damaging their performance in the afternoon, before no doubt impacting upon their evening too.

When we are tired and negatively stressed, we worsen the situation by being attracted to the calorific and high-sugar snacks that give us a quick boost but ultimately see us crash all too speedily.

Take breakfast. You haul yourself out of bed and pour yourself a strong coffee, perhaps aided and abetted by some sugar-fuelled cereal. You reach work, but your early surge has already dimmed. That caffeine is coursing through your bloodstream triggering the release of the stress hormone: cortisol. This state of artificial stress and readiness can prove exhausting. You have no reserves left for teaching your classes.

I admit my hypocrisy here. I am an inveterate coffee drinker. I love the stuff. I can't shake the habit, but I am getting better at managing it. I have eliminated sugar from my coffee and cut down on the sugary snacks. I now eat fruit during the day for a natural glucose boost. It has been a steady and small change in my diet, but such marginal gains matter.

A check on the Web will see you find a cornucopia of advice about a balanced nutritional diet. Simple habits, like drinking more water, or substituting the chocolate and cakes for fruit, are within our reach. They will have the attendant benefit of feeding us with the fuel that can help us strive for greater competence and confidence.

Sleep

It is Sunday night (I bet you know where I am going with this) and your lesson planning isn't quite finished, but you have done enough. You have ticked a few other jobs off your to-do list and you aim for a relatively early night. After an hour of lying in bed, turning endlessly, desperate to claim some sleep, your negative stress level rises like heat. You stop looking at the clock and you know that the rest of your week will not catch up and claim back these lost hours.

It is the fear and loathing known by teachers the world over. Even if you enjoy teaching and you find working with your colleagues and students a profound pleasure, you can still experience this unique feeling of anxiety that clings to Sunday nights and to the ends of our school holidays.

Again, we need to recognise what our body is doing and why. If we are to live until ninety years of age, then we will spend an estimated thirty-two of those years asleep. Clearly, sleeping is no indulgence. It is essential for replenishing our energies, charging our creativity and readying ourselves for our classes and our colleagues.

Too easily, our necessary seven to nine hours of quality sleep gets whittled down to short and broken attempts. The vital replenishment for our body and brain provided by a restful sleep is integral for you to fend off school stresses. We need an average of eight hours – some of us need a little more, some a little less (indeed, teenagers need a whopping nine hours sleep a night to function effectively at school). No amount of willpower can make up for a lack of sleep when we consistently lose out on it.

So what can you do to battle that Sunday night negative stress and to get the sleep you need? Try these simple strategies:

- Aim for regular sleeping hours, with nightly cues and calming rituals, like a good book before bed etc. If work thoughts invade your attempts to sleep, then make a ritual of completing a list for the next day to soothe your anxieties and to let go.
- Keep your bedroom a technology free zone. Emails receive a definitive no.
- Avoid caffeine four to six hours before sleep.
- Avoid alcohol and high sugar snacks near sleep.
- Cut out napping after six pm.

Combatting stress

- Don't toss and turn endlessly. If you are still awake after a twenty-minute span, then get out of bed, undertake a relaxing activity, like reading, then try sleeping again soon after.

Sleep is like depositing money in a bank. The interest on your account builds as you sleep in a good regular pattern, but the converse is sadly true. Given a few nights of poor sleep, you become deeply indebted and your brain can struggle to replenish its precious reserves. Getting into a good sleep pattern, with little rituals to convince your busy brain that sleep is afoot, is crucial.

The comfort of crowds and colleagues

'A problem shared is a problem halved' is the apple-pie-sweet aphorism. Alas, the opposite is also true. I know many a teacher whose sanctuary is the classroom and whose stresses are to be found squarely at the door of their colleagues. Some teaching colleagues, like every profession, can prove a drain on our emotional resources. Still, having a network of colleagues supporting you will help reduce your negative stress in most cases.

When our colleagues mirror our emotions, our stress levels can actually decrease. Let's put that into context. Preparing to talk in front of the entire school staff when you are a quivering wreck is a fear that plagues many teachers' minds. If you ready yourself accompanied by a seasoned teacher who is wholly assured, then their attempts to becalm you may flounder. Instead, if a colleague were to mirror your fears, by way of similarity, then they provide a helpful buffer for that shot of stress firing your way.[7]

Similarity breeds contentment, and helping others is a great way to mitigate your own negative stresses. Having friends and colleagues at school who share our concerns and fears can help stave off some of our more debilitating worries, thereby providing us with the conditions to focus on taking risks and developing our professional practice.

The solutions we seek are most often in our social circle. Love and friendship can help conquer our negative stress. You will have heard of 'fight or flight', but 'tend and befriend' is an equally common response to stress. Everyone knows how a simple hug can make our stresses flood away. If you don't, or you haven't experienced this phenomenon, then you are probably in dire need of a good hug.

You now have the scientific basis to hug your fellow teachers. Use it wisely.

Write and reflect

For over three years I have written a blog about teaching and education. Billowed and buffeted by the day job, I wanted a place to record my ideas, unleash my corked rants and think about how I could get a little better and more confident.

The struggle for time, repeated in this book as the lived experience of most teachers, would appear to crush the argument for writing to enhance your confidence. Surely we don't have time or energy for pursuits like writing? Although perceived by most as an extra 'job', it actually made me feel more effective and more efficient. Over time, by forcing myself to reflect and giving me an audience to connect with about my daily practice, I became more confident in what I do.

It is counter-intuitive – surely writing after a long day at school was *more* work – but it didn't *feel* like it. That made all the difference. It was, unknowingly at first, a way to reflect and better manage my daily stresses.

This feeling was supported by a Harvard Business School research paper on 'how the 15-minute activity of writing and reflecting at the end of the working day may make you more successful'.[8] Paradoxically, the act of regular blogging felt like a time-saver. In another quite startling study, the act of writing about a recent trauma actually saw the trauma wound heal faster.[9] Clearly, the psychological impact of writing and reflection can prove a potent boost for us all.

Get a life

Much has been said about the importance of getting a work/life balance; however, I think we need to rethink this divide. Instead of perceiving the tension between our work and our home life, we should instead recognise that teaching is an integral part of our lives (though we should carefully manage its presence in our home).

Of course, our schoolwork should not consume our home lives. Consider our sense of balance if we committed the time and effort to organising our time with our family and friends like we did to completing our essential projects at work. Perhaps we need to take having fun more seriously.

Too many teachers, who are also parents, in aiming to better the lives of their student brethren, forget to tend to their own children. The guilt and anxiety that can build isn't healthy for anyone. It is about the judicious balance of two competing urges and the recognition that you cannot neatly complete every facet of your professional life, but you can better manage it and yourself.

The power of control

We know that our 'locus of control' – the extent to which we believe we can control the events around us – is essential for our sense of self-confidence. If we do not believe that we make a difference to our students' lives, even if there are social factors that make the likelihood of success a challenge, then we may struggle to maintain our best efforts when experiencing negative stress.

Take a simple test.

- *Do you believe you can control student behaviour in your classroom?*
- *Do you believe you can change what the head teacher thinks of you?*
- *Do you believe you can control the chaotic home life of one of your students?*

We must know that we cannot control everything. That seemingly obvious fact can sometimes liberate us of the subtly corrosive guilt that can attend our thinking. We can too often think in absolutes. Notions of absolutes like 'never' and 'always' are unhelpful. Sometimes we will succeed in our task; sometimes we will fail. Both may stem from our very best efforts.

We can better control ourselves, our internal 'locus of control', which will go some way to helping us manage our response to the external factors that we inevitably have less control over.

What we must be is flexible and agile in the face of our daily stresses – both good and bad.

We will have days when our best efforts flounder and our best-laid plans will go wrong. And yet we needn't respond with catastrophic thinking. We can still regain control of the behaviour of our students. With good teaching, we can change the assumptions of our head teacher. With an unmitigated regard for our students, we can bring some degree of calm to the chaos of their lives, at least while they are with us.

We needn't pursue optimism to the point of naiveté, or refuse to countenance the truth of a bad situation, but we can take care to be conscious of our own thinking. We know that seeing everything positively can make us little more than some Pollyanna character and can inhibit our pursuit of genuine self-improvement, but being hopeful is natural fuel for a teacher.

A bad lesson can prove, well, just a bad lesson. In the face of daily but ultimately temporary failures, we can still retain our sense of control and perspective, holding onto our long-term goals and responsibilities that drive us forward. In the clutch of circumstance, for good or ill, we can still be confident that we can come back tomorrow and be better. Just as our confidence can ebb, with effort and commitment, we can make it flow once more.

In ending this chapter, it is important to note that you should not feel under pressure to undertake a raft of the ideas from this chapter, or indeed this book, all at once. That would prove counterproductive. Instead, we should seek to do one small change well, making it a habit and building from there. These small changes can release some negative stress and accumulate into something powerful that supports your daily work as a teacher.

IN SHORT...

- Stress is a natural bedfellow for teachers. Better recognising the signs of negative stress, in both ourselves and in others, is of crucial importance. Though too often we cannot control our working hours, or the whims of education policymakers, we can better control ourselves and be mindful of our emotions and our stress levels.
- We need to recognise the signs of negative stress and **HALT**.

- We should recognise that stress can be a positive force and work upon thinking about how it can enhance our performance.
- Seemingly unimportant actions, like straightening our posture, or going for a short walk, can bolster our resistance to the storms of negative stress that can occur in the classroom and the staffroom.
- By undertaking these actions, and by taking care of ourselves and others, we can retain that all-important sense of control over our working lives.

Notes

1 UK Government, Department for Work and Pensions (2013), 'An evaluation of the statement of fitness for work (fit note): Quantitative survey of fit notes'. [Online]. Available at: www.gov.uk/government/uploads/system/uploads/attachment_data/file/207526/841summ.pdf (Accessed: 27 October 2014).
2 UK Department of Education (2014), 'Teachers' workload diary survey 2013', Research report (February 2014).
3 Skaalvik, E.M. and Skaalvik, S. (2010), 'Teacher self-efficacy and teacher burnout: A study of relations', *Teaching and Teacher Education*, 26: 1059–1069.
4 Gervais, R.L. and Hockey, G.R.L. (2005), 'Daily hassles, daily uplifts, sleep loss and stress', Proceedings of the *British Psychological Society*, 13 (2): 153–154.
5 Keller, A., Litzelman, K., Wisk, L.E., Maddox, T., Cheng, E.R., Creswell., P.D. and Witt, W.P. (2012), 'Does the perception that stress affects health matter? The association with health and mortality', *Health Psychology*, 31(5): 677–684.
6 Nair, S., Sagar, M., Sollers, J., Consedine, N. and Broadbent, E. (2014), 'Do slumped and upright postures affect stress responses? A randomized trial', *Health Psychology*, 34 (6): 632–641.
7 Sara, S.M., Townsend, S.M., Kim, H.S. and Mesquita, B. (2014), 'Are You Feeling What I'm Feeling? Emotional

Similarity Buffers Stress'. *Social Psychological and Personality Science*, 5 (5): 526–533. [Online]. Available at: http://ppw.kuleuven.be/home/english/research/cscp/documents/mesquita/townsend-kim-mesquita-2013-are-you-feeling-what-im.pdf (Accessed: 5 June 2015).

8   Di Stefano, G., Gino, F., Pisano, G.P. and Staats, B. (2014), 'Learning by thinking: How reflection aids performance', Harvard Business School Technology and Operations Management Unit Working Paper No. 14–93.

9   Weinman, J., Ebrecht, M., Scott, S., Walburn, J. and Dyson, M. (2008), 'Enhanced wound healing after emotional disclosure intervention'. *British Journal of Health Psychology*, 13: 95–102. doi: 10.1348/135910707X251207.

8 The performance of teaching

Apparently, the number one fear people face each day is the fear of public speaking. It is a fear that even comes before a fear of dying.

Consider that for a moment: rather than giving a eulogy at a funeral, we would rather be lying in the coffin. Our confidence in our capacity for public speaking, so critical to being a successful teacher, is clearly in need of a boost.

Consider the great public speakers of the last century. What names are called to your mind? I bet you envision great people and confident public speakers.

Did Winston Churchill make your list? Few people in human history have raised public speaking to such an art form, making inspired speeches to rouse a nation and

125

deeply affect so many people. And yet, Winston Churchill lacked all confidence in his speaking ability. Famously, his early pre-war speeches fell on dull ears and failed to inspire. Such chastening failure didn't deter Winston, as we now know with the clear view of hindsight.

Churchill's stammer and lisp severely hampered his confidence in giving speeches. He went about conquering his neurotic fears by researching great orators; devising his own unique style and deviating from typical speech patterns that would see him stammer and stop. He created elaborate preparatory routines. Churchill would script his speeches meticulously by hand, even to the point of adding in stage directions.

In short, he undertook the difficult course of deliberate practice common to all experts.

He struggled successfully and overcame his stammer and his lisp. His unusual choice of syntax, a memorable trademark, was an artful response to help avoid the tricky rhythms of everyday speech, but it became a speciality. Through dogged effort and practice, he transformed what was a personal weakness into a towering strength that would echo throughout human history.

Churchill is no one-off. Throughout history the story is repeated. The greatest orator of ancient Greece, Demosthenes, also had to overcome a debilitating speech impediment. With the unique strategy of placing small stones in his mouth, to help him practice enunciating his words, he worked hard at his speech-making prowess until he had honed his celebrated style.

As we can see from these great public speakers from history, confidence isn't some warm and fuzzy feeling, but instead it is a series of concrete behaviours that we practice and enact with effort and increasing skill.

Developing self-confidence in our performance can prove as physical as heaving dumb-bells in a weight room and its impact can be just as exhausting, but, ultimately, we must make the effort to both literally, and figuratively, 'walk tall' and talk with confidence.

So what are the physical 'moves' to appear confident and to 'walk tall'? It is about standing up straight, relaxing your shoulders and slightly widening your stance so that you get a solid 'base' from which to project your voice. It is about making eye contact and using open hand gestures. It is about speaking with a lower pitch and an ever so slightly quieter and slower voice than you would do so in normal speech.

We know that people who appear more physically confident are trusted, and people instinctively equate extroversion with competence and expertise. Too often, by talking quickly, too quietly and verbally discounting ourselves, thereby self-sabotaging what we say, we commit a self-fulfilling prophecy. We dislike public speaking, so we reveal our discomfort and nervousness with hurried gestures, or saying 'sorry' unnecessarily. It isn't just what we say and how we say it, but, most crucially, it is what people hear and see. Our students and our colleagues hear and see our confidence in subtle unison.

Smiling is priming

When I began as a teacher I was given the very common but highly dubious advice to 'not smile before Christmas'. The idea is probably shorthand for establishing some firm rules nice and early, but it is ill-conceived advice all the same. Indeed, we should do the opposite: we should exercise the immense power of smiling.

The reality is that we couldn't possibly stop smiling if we wanted to. We begin smiling even before we were born. It is fundamental to our ability to communicate effectively and it spans every culture across the globe. Of course, we would not wish to be confused with some mad clown smiling incessantly, but a genuine smile goes a long way.

We are all conditioned for subliminal priming from a simple smile. Just a flicker of a smile toward a student can make a difference. As Gladwell stated, we make 'blink' style judgements that are instantaneous and often undertaken even before we recognise our conscious thoughts.

Students are more inclined to see their teacher in a more positive light with a smile. Implicitly, explanations can become more interesting and feedback more valuable. The opposite is also true. A smiling student can be treated more leniently than a student who isn't, as they too are deemed more trustworthy, sincere and honourable than their non-smiling peers.[1] In short, the simple human act of smiling can transform how we feel and can even help fuel our confidence.[2]

Smile and the whole word smiles with you and it can make a difference in the classroom.

The power of gesture and confident body language

Like smiling, an instantaneous gesture can prove momentary, but it can have lasting effects on our students. Gesture has long since been studied for its social power. They are instinctive and most often prove unconscious acts.

All this talk of a physical 'performance' can draw complaints for being inauthentic – we should be ourselves, not faking some act. Though we should be wary of reducing ourselves to some painted marionette, we can recognise that many of our behaviours can be learnt and that there is a degree of faking confidence before we truly become confident in our teaching practice.

We know that we think with our bodies: our thoughts and our emotions are entwined and our body communicates them both – sometimes beyond our control. Our grasp of language is intimately entwined and supported by our physical gestures. Often, our confidence, or lack thereof, is betrayed in our subtle acts of non-verbal communication, such as our hand masking our face, or nervous tugs at our clothing.

Even the memory of what we teach is enhanced by some simple gestures.[3] I quickly think of the 'robot arms' deployed by my little boy when he is segmenting his phonic sounds. Gesture does not only help students learn and remember explanations better, it also can convey your assured control to your audience.

Gestures can prove idiosyncratic, but some prove universal. I have watched a teacher silence a cacophony with a slow raised hand, raise a cheer from a thumbs up and refocus an entire class of lively students with a steady shake of their head. Slow and deliberate hand gestures can convey subtly different messages. Open hands, with palms up can prove inviting and warm; hands behind your back, held loosely and with ease, can convey you are without fear.

Take a simple thumbs up or a clap. These can inspire momentary acts of excitement; confirmation and validation that lingers in the minds of our students far more than we ever remember ourselves. A small head nod and leaning forward when a student gives a good answer to a question sends lots of positive signals to our students. It is actually surprising how potent these micro signals can prove.

These small acts of non-verbal communication matter, but they often work on a subliminal level and therefore we too easily ignore their importance.

If I consider for a moment some of the many expert teachers I have had the privilege to observe, a common feature of their performance was a sense of serenity, a calmness of delivery and movement. The message, almost always implicit, to each student: I am confident. I am calm. I am in utter control.

The aforementioned *Lean In*, by Sheryl Sandberg, focused more specifically upon the professional confidence of women, but this was conveyed physically too. The very act of leaning in proved for Sandberg a subtle but important symbol of physical confidence and of assertiveness. She was of course right.

Our sense of confidence and performance proves a very physical act. Smiling, open hand gestures, consistent eye contact, mirroring body language, leaning forward in a non-threatening way, can all convey our physical confidence. We should be mindful of their impact.

Now, picture Rodin's famous sculpture: *The Thinker*. Visualise that pose, the hand cupped under the chin, the brow furrowed. This sculpture is so iconic because it symbolically epitomises such deep thinking. We too can convey those messages to encourage the behaviour we want.

We can encourage excitement with speedy nods and a subtle bounce on our heels, before then seeking slow and thorough-going thinking with a mere finger on the chin. A thumb up signal can affect a student tackling a tricky mathematics problem. In a moment, we can prime our students just how we want them to learn.

We sometimes have our own repertoire of body language that is often unconsciously enacted. I have watched teachers slumped against walls, symbolically hiding behind desks and closing their body with arms folded and worse, on many occasions. What is your repertoire? You likely cannot articulate it. Film yourself and turn off the volume for a short time and you will quickly diagnose your physical 'moves'. It can prove an enlightening experience.

Let's stop all this reading and thinking, and take a moment to get physical. Here are some simple moves: stand tall, place your legs apart, clench your fists with firmness and place them onto your hips. There...you are now 'power posing'. Keep it for a minute or two.

Now, what you have done, or are doing (if you are not doing it then you are a spoilsport), is based upon the hugely popular research by American Professor Amy Cuddy. Her *TED* talk on how 'Your Body Language Shapes Who You Are'[4] relates her research that 'power posing' helped improve presentation performance in interview scenarios. This alluring message has so far reached an audience of over 27 million at the time of writing.

So, shouldn't we all be power posing prior to our lessons?

An audience for finding the solutions to our performance anxiety is clear in the vast numbers viewing the *TED* talk on Cuddy's posing. Alas, Cuddy's power posing is no quick fix. A larger study, undertaken at the University of Zurich,[5] replicated Cuddy's work and showed that the 'power pose' had little of the promised transformative properties. It may temporarily inflate our mood, instilling some temporary confidence, but no doubt the authentic confidence of interview preparedness, alongside some conscious approaches to our physical performance, should be our aim when looking to succeed on interview day.

Despite the rather grand claims, Professor Cuddy's research no doubt chimes with our instincts about physical confidence. Sometimes becoming confident requires acting confidently to others.

We should be wary of quick fix confidence tricks, like singular poses to give us authority, but we should remain conscious of our physical communication and its power. I am not saying our performance matters more than what we actually say, but we can harmonise the conviction of what we say with the physicality of how we say it.

That big speech to our teacher colleagues

It is an irony for many teachers that they spend much of their working lives speaking to large groups of students, but the notion of speaking to a large group of their colleagues fills them with fear and loathing. In front of our peers our self-consciousness is heightened and for some it can prove debilitating. No amount of power posing wipes away that deep-seated fear.

We suffer what is known as the *spotlight effect*. That is to say, we believe that people are focused more on us than they actually are, or that they easily recognise our nervousness. The truth is that people don't recognise the nervousness that we assume they do[6] and that only with overt self-sabotage, when we begin to verbally draw attention to our worries or our flaws, do people actually notice our mental state of nerve-jangling fear.

This way of viewing the world is nothing new. Roman Emperor Marcus Aurelius mused in his *Meditations* why man sets less value on his own opinion of himself than on the opinion of others. We should consider this ancient wisdom and not be beholden to our phantom fear of the spotlight when faced with large groups of our colleagues.

As we imagine we are under the spotlight, we hedge and we hesitate with our speech and our movements and gestures can become hurried and more erratic. Our performance becomes a self-fulfilling prophecy of nervousness and fear. As we associate high confidence with expertise, the opposite is true when we betray our fears and our lack of confidence.

Why is being a confident speaker important? Rightly or wrongly, we believe confident speakers more,[7] trusting in their self-belief and seeming expertise. Not only that, such confidence is valued and trusted even more in group settings.[8] This obviously matters in the classroom when trust is so essential to listening and learning. Outside the classroom too, working with our teacher colleagues, the benefits are clear.

Unsurprisingly, research shows that people judge speakers as less anxious than they judge themselves.[9] They are likely obsessing over their own performance and anxieties, fearing their next experience under the spotlight. So the results are in – we should speak to our colleagues safe in the knowledge that they aren't paying us the close attention we assume!

Once more, we must act with the grace of the swan, though our true thoughts, hidden from plain sight, are figuratively kicking with anxious intent beneath the surface.

How can we approach that big speech to our colleagues so that grace and confidence prove more likely than fear? Albert Bandura's guide to self-efficacy once again proves instructive. We need to interpret our signs of physical stress – fast breathing, a rapidly beating heart and more – as our bodies ramping up the excitement ready to perform.

It is worth reminding ourselves of the notion of courage. Speaking to groups of people, students or our fellow teachers, requires lots of it. The word courage comes with the Latin prefix 'cor', meaning heart. Public speaking is an act of showing our heart. If it is beating frantically before we start, then it should prove only a reminder of our courage in standing up and speaking.

We will be unlikely to convince ourselves to be calm. The distance between our racing heartbeat and our desired calmness is so far that we cannot con ourselves. Instead, we need to reappraise our anxiety as excitement.[10] Even telling ourselves to get excited (quietly, we don't want to appear mad) can seize a modicum of control for us that can help stabilise our performance.

Of course, the pessimism and self-doubt that attends our big speech serves another positive purpose. The defensive pessimism we suffer actually drives us toward preparing ourselves more thoroughly. We all know the decisive impact of a deadline on our performance. We have all begun working on a Sunday evening with the stark light of Monday morning driving us through the tedium and the temptation to procrastinate.

The performance of teaching

A confident performance rests on the bedrock of preparation.

Practising our talk and scripting it, at least the skeleton structure of the talk, can help reduce anxiety and build our confidence. By having elements of what we are going to say committed to memory automatically, we are freed up to concentrate on the more challenging elements of our performance, like making conscious gestures, movements and even breathing effectively. If we have prepared what we are going to say, it allows us to give eye contact to our audience, so crucial in connecting and garnering interest, rather than having to rely on reading from our notes or a script.

Small details matter. Ensure that you are well hydrated so that you don't have a mouth that feels as dry and arid as the Gobi desert. Get some rest in preparation for a big talk. The more tired you are, the more your individual voice patterns will diminish. A tired and flat talk is good for no one. As we know, a small dose of anxiety can enhance our performance, but if we experience too much then it saps us of vital energy reserves.

Perhaps we shouldn't attempt to be calm before the big talk, but we should aim to make our breathing consistent and consciously slower than we normally would. The 'Alexander technique' is a well-established method for doing just that. A vast array of videos on this technique can be found on the Internet. Essentially, this breathing exercise promotes a good balanced posture that is essential for clear and confident speaking.

Standing tall and straightening your posture really matters on two counts. Your body language conveys confidence and also it allows you to breath more deeply, subtly slowing down your talk – another crucial indicator of natural confidence.

Don't worry – you don't need to strike another 'power pose' – but you do need to put in a confident performance.

The little voice in your head

The notion of self-talk can make me feel a little uneasy. It can veer perilously near the falsity of self-help books: telling yourself that you are the world's best teacher and the like. And yet, self-talk doesn't have to be the remit of the slick self-help guru. Most self-talk is wholly reasonable and of the, 'I really need to prepare for this big talk', or the, 'remember to breathe and drink water' variety.

Without warning, such a voice can quite easily cast doubt upon our thinking and action. Being conscious and aware of our mood, relaying positive messages to ourselves, can prove a pragmatic and professional response to our work. Many sports scientists swear by the power of visualisation and self-talk, and I do know teachers who spend their preparatory time in the morning running through mental pictures of their prospective lessons.

In essence, framing such a fear-fuelling event like talking to a mass of adults as an exciting event requires some self-talk. Recognising our stresses and rethinking our physical responses is a variation on self-talk. We simply need to reality-test our emotions, asking: what is the worst that could happen? Am I jumping to negative conclusions? What benefits am I receiving from talking? We can avoid catastrophic thinking if we are conscious of our mental foibles.

The best self-talk will remind us of the following essentials when giving that big talk:

- Nerves are natural and essential to sharpen our thinking.
- People are not shining the harsh spotlight on us that we think: they're too busy fumbling over their own fears and neuroses to notice.
- Our colleagues are usually rooting for us to do well.
- Slow down your talk, look around and aim to smile.

The performance of teaching

- Don't use self-sabotaging talk with your audience – people often only notice a slip up when you tell them you have done so.
- Practice until it *looks* natural, even it is doesn't *feel* like it is.

We can even make use of some controlled catastrophic thinking as deployed in the ancient wisdom from the Stoic philosophers. The Stoics would consider the worst-case scenario; even contemplating that alleged number two fear – death – when seeking to better manage their thoughts and feelings. We needn't go so far, but we can consider these worst-case scenarios of our public speaking for what they are – not remotely as bad as we think.

We must keep things in perspective and consider the absurdity of our fear of public speaking over death.

Let's jump out of the coffin and perform that eulogy.

IN SHORT...

- How we perform and act when we speak to students and our colleagues requires confidence. Ernest Hemingway described courage as 'grace under pressure'. I think this is a very apt description of the teacher performance in the classroom.
- We should be conscious of the marginal details of our physical performance, like smiling and our gestures.
- Preparation for a big talk is key, including preparing to think about our physical and psychological responses. Aim for excitement over anxiety.
- Remember, the spotlight we imagine we are under when speaking does not match the interests or imaginings of our audience. We can cut ourselves some slack. People are likely too busy obsessing about their own morbid fear of public speaking.

Notes

1   LaFrance, M. and Hecht, M.A. (1995), 'Why smiles generate leniency', *Personality and Social Psychology Bulletin*, 21 (3): 207–214.

2   Critchley, H.H. and Nagai, Y. (2012), 'How emotions are shaped by bodily states', *Emotion Review*, 4: 163.

3   Novack, M.A., Eliza, L., Congdon, E.L., Hemani-Lopez, N. and Goldin-Meadow, S. (2014), 'From action to abstraction: Using the hands to learn math', *Psychological Science*, published online 6 February 2014.

4   Cuddy, A. (2012), TED Talks: 'Your body language shapes who you are'. [Online]. Available at: www.ted.com/talks/ amy_cuddy_your_body_language_shapes_who_you_ are?language=en (Accessed: 11 December 2014).

5   Ranehill, E. et al. (2015), 'Assessing the robustness of power posing: No effect on hormones and risk tolerance in a large sample of men and women', *Psychological Science* OnlineFirst, doi:10.1177/0956797614553946.

6   Clevenger, T.J. (1959), 'A synthesis of experimental research in stage fright'. *Quarterly Journal of Speech*, 45: 135–159.

7   Penrod, S.D. and Cutler, B.L. (1995), 'Witness confidence and witness accuracy: Assessing their forensic relation', *Psychology, Public Policy, and Law*, 1: 817–845.

8   Zarnoth, P. and Sniezek, J.A. (1997), 'The social influence of confidence in group decision making', *Journal of Experimental Social Psychology*, 33: 345–366.

9   Savitsky, K. and Gilovich, T. (2003), 'The illusion of transparency and the alleviation of speech anxiety', *Journal of Experimental Social Psychology*, 39: 601–625.

10 Wood-Brooks, A. (2014), 'Get excited: Reappraising pre-performance anxiety as excitement', *Journal of Experimental Psychology: American Psychological Association*, 143 (3): 1144–1158.

9 Managing student behaviour

Our students crave confidence and trust in their teacher. They seek it out, listening for it in the words we speak and looking to read it in our every gesture and movement.

We send out messages all day long that are stored and accumulated by our students. Our students loathe mixed messages. When we say 'Any questions?' but we then don't pause and wait for a response because we don't really want any questions, our students lose a degree of trust. Each and every interaction makes up our relationship, and that relationship can define the behaviour of our students.

The craving our students exhibit for confidence and trust in their teacher is largely grown from our being caring and consistent.

We can create a safe classroom that is founded on trust and care, yet we know that students can face battles outside of school that drain their capacity to trust. Every once in a while the bleak personal stories of our students' lives are opened up to us like a drawer of knives. We get a brief glimpse into personal prisons that children shouldn't ever experience.

Many of our students' negative behaviours in our classroom become better understood when we hear their story: the missing homework, the rudeness, the mood swings, or the inability to look us in the eye when we speak to them. It never excuses the damaging behaviours that they commit, with other children often caught in the middle of those vicious salvos, but it does illuminate and explain their origins.

I think about a recent student of mine: let's call her Jessica for the sake of her privacy. Only recently I heard the latest update about her life since leaving school. To describe her family as 'broken' would not do justice to the chaos it had wrought upon her young self, and continued to do, beyond her removal from school.

I was reminded of the mix of emotions I felt when she left my class. My instinctive feeling that I had personally failed her was mingled with guilt for being somewhat relieved at her permanently leaving my class. I had momentarily feasted on the optimism that a change of setting, and school, could better suit her needs; that a new school would provide her with a fresh start.

Predictably, a rumoured update about Jessica laid waste to my hopes.

We do our very best each day for students like Jessica, despite the most trying of circumstances. We give them unconditional regard; we set the boundaries they have needed all along; we attempt to lift them with our rocket-high expectations. Despite this, the complex circumstances in the lives of our students like Jessica undermine our attempts to improve their behaviour and to develop their confidence. They inhibit the capacity for trust in us as a teacher: a chief ingredient in providing the conditions for developing a successful relationship.

In 1974, the eminent psychologist Walter Mischel conducted a famous experiment: *The Marshmallow Test*. Two fluffy cubes of sugar would come to symbolise a child's capacity for self-control. It was a simply designed test: a child was given one marshmallow. They were sat in a room for a short time and if they could fend off eating the single marshmallow then they were granted a second marshmallow as a reward. It was a classic exercise in impulse control and delayed gratification.

For children like Jessica, her environment was so unstable that she would struggle to not eat the marshmallow. The patent lack of stability and trust in her life would likely see her impulses take control, possibly imitating some of the damaging behaviours from her chaotic home life.

Celeste Kidd, a researcher from the University of Rochester, imitated Mischel's classic marshmallow test. Her study on 'rational snacking'[1] showed that when the people giving the marshmallows proved unreliable, then children were more likely to eat the marshmallow. This simple experiment exposed a profound human truth: trust can drive our behaviour. It certainly influences the behaviour of our students.

It follows that when we are considering the best behaviour management of our students, each teacher should ask: how will I earn the trust of my students? What actions will I undertake with fairness and consistency?

You may rightly question: what about those students who misbehave despite the best circumstances in their home lives? Frankly, there are many more of these students than there are students who are suffering from bad fortune like Jessica. And yet, the core principles of confident behaviour management remain the same for all students, in any classroom:

- Students need a teacher who is consistent, reliable and trustworthy.
- They need a teacher who develops a relationship founded upon trust.
- They need a teacher who calmly and consistently models the behaviours they expect.
- They need a teacher who relentlessly makes their high expectations of behaviour clear to all.

In short, all students need *confidence* in their teacher.

Just like adults, and teachers, self-confident students better persevere and maintain their effort through difficulties and challenges.[2] What develops between the teacher and the student becomes a relationship built upon reciprocity – we share confidence in one another.

Developing relationships with our students is of course our first priority. We can then establish a climate of trust without a reliance on fear. This isn't necessarily about proving ourselves as their new favourite teacher. Too easily, a focus on trust and developing a relationship becomes confused with being liked and not establishing the boundaries for the good behaviour that are needed. The kindest act we could ever commit for our students would be to give them the safety conferred by explicit boundaries of how they should behave.

We are ultimately their role models in their school lives and beyond. We face the marshmallow test of self-control each day too. When we are stressed, tired and strained by over-work, we need to maintain our consistency, our control and our self-confidence.

If we are to manage the behaviour of others successfully, we must first be successful in managing our own. This necessitates being consciously aware of our language, the non-verbal messages we convey along with our words, as well as possessing an acute understanding of the needs of all of our students.

We need to build rigorous and relentless routines. School-wide systems and high standards of support are crucial, but consistency begins at home. Creating clear and consistent rules sits comfortably with a climate of unmitigated regard for our students.

Confident control

It all sounds so easy. Of course, if it were so easy, then the challenging behaviour of our students would not prove so universally damaging to teacher confidence.

A common story is played out in every school, seemingly in every country. In self-defence, we attribute any student misbehaviour to our students and factors outside of our control. Anxiety about failing to manage our classroom cuts deep at our sense of pride. This is then compounded by our not asking for help. Before we know it, we can find ourselves crashing to the brink of burnout.

As we know, a strange truth about teaching is that it can prove a remarkably private, and even secretive, profession. As my former colleague and fellow English teacher, Helen Day, honestly stated: 'It is okay to come out as struggling with teaching approaches like questioning or feedback, but to be seen to do the same for behaviour management would be interpreted as weak.' As Helen describes, too many teachers are driven by fear and bury their issues.

In too many schools, teachers would fear for their jobs if they were open about the truth of the poor student behaviour in their classrooms, regardless of whether circumstances were patently against them. Even in good schools, with effective behaviour management systems and supportive school leaders, struggles are fought in quiet desperation in too many classrooms. The unofficial law of silence can wear away at our confidence.

We think that the teacher across the hallway is dealing with misbehaviour just fine, bolstered by many teachers claiming as much, in order to protect their own professional pride. Our psychological demons prey on our insecurities and our brain plays memory tricks on us. Ground down by our anxieties, we can too easily become overcome with negative stress.

In my first few years of teaching it was behaviour management, or more accurately my lack of it, that nearly cast me on the well-trodden path out of teaching. It was a terribly lonely experience, despite having friends and colleagues who provided much support. In an act of self-preservation, I limited knowledge of my struggles to as few people as possible.

With the vivid clarity of high-definition television, I can remember such instances of behavioural chaos in my classroom. One such incident was no doubt a turning point for me as a teacher.

To paint the scene would prove something of a parody of a gothic tale: rain lashing against a rickety temporary classroom and the darkness of an English winter gathering in. Late in the week, at the end of another gruelling school day, my GCSE English class were running me ragged.

My instructions were clanging into the corners of the room unheard. I made the weak assertion that each of my thirty-two students could choose whether they wanted to complete the essay writing task or not. I had virtually given up. Unsurprisingly, thirty-one students chose to talk and not take me up on the offer of writing their essay.

I slumped in my teacher chair, seriously contemplating my next career move – one most likely outside the classroom and the teaching profession. At home that night,

I considered my next steps and whether teaching was for me. Too many failures, grinding tiredness and student misbehaviour, across the span of a few terms, had left me with little to no confidence in my ability to teach. The threads of my self-confidence had worn perilously thin and were close to breaking point.

The next day, I stood in front of the group and spoke of my deep disappointment. I then kept them all in class for an extra half hour (as the lesson was, fortuitously for me, situated directly before lunchtime) to do the work they had missed whilst chatting the afternoon before.

Every student was kept behind except one. The one student, who had chosen to work away the afternoon before, Natalie Elliott, had been spared my complaints and disappointment and she was sent off for her lunch as usual.

It is no exaggeration to say that it was Natalie's behaviour, her choosing to write her essay whilst all around her were talking away and wasting time, that gave me some small hope to cling to. I sat with the rest at lunchtime for thirty minutes in near pristine silence with the group. I gave them a talk that I had stewed over for hours the night before.

It wasn't the end of my behaviour management struggles by any means, but it was a turning point for me. Winning that small battle gave me some vital confidence to continue.

In retrospect, though I didn't realise it then, it was a crucial *expert experience.* It gave me just enough confidence to stave off burnout and to continue with committed effort through my all too frequent failures. With the value of hindsight, those memories now bolster my confidence. I now have a distinct sense of control, but it was hard earned and I was given a great deal of support along the way.

My training had dismally failed to prepare me for confidently managing the behaviour of all my classes. It would take some years, gathering that knowledge piece by piece, often in quiet desperation, scouring books about behaviour, watching every video on the topic I could find, whilst picking up vital tips from my more experienced colleagues.

Over time, I came to develop a repertoire of learnt behaviours that would become a visible manifestation of confident behaviour management.

In a pleasing plot twist to finish the misbehaviour anecdote that is so scorched on my memory, Natalie went on to great success in school. I went on to teach her A-level English Language and she proved the first of my students to score full marks in the examination. Then, nearly a decade later, she became a teacher colleague of mine.

She cannot remember one moment of that cold and wet afternoon, and now, I am sure she has her own afternoon battles to win, but I can remember it like it was yesterday.

The conditions for confident behaviour management

In Shakespeare's *Othello*, Cassio famously bewailed: 'Reputation, reputation, reputation!' Clearly, he understood the teeth-gnashing anxieties of teachers who have had their reputation stained by a difficult class. It happens to the best of us, inexperienced and experienced alike, as our teacher reputation can be won or lost each year of our teaching career.

The act of confident behaviour management begins even before students enter the room. Your reputation precedes you. It walks in and sits in the teacher's chair before you even turn the door handle.

Do you stick to the school rules and sanctions? Do you follow through with what you say will happen if students misbehave? In short, do students see you as a confident teacher? They make such judgements quickly and their decisions matter.

If you don't stick to the known school rules, then students will act. There is nothing so certain as students smelling fear and seizing the initiative from a cowed teacher; such knowledge spreads like a virus. There is nothing so predictable as a teenager seeking out the unfairness of rules being inconsistently applied.

Alas, a reputation can take a great deal of time to establish and overnight success stories prove rare things. That being said, we can accelerate the process by conveying assurance and certainty. This can be asserted relatively quickly through a combination of physicality, a consistency of action, and an utter clarity when asserting our expectations.

I often hear teacher advice to establish the right 'climate for learning', or to build the right 'culture' for positive behaviour, or even more vague, 'you need to develop *presence*'. The problem is that such advice can prove maddeningly woolly and unhelpful. Instead, we need to chunk the notion of 'climate for learning' into something tangible that we can establish with a sequence of 'moves' – clear, consistent, and often, very physical moves.

We know that students make snap judgements about the capacity of their teacher in the blink of an eye. Simply pausing and giving students a momentary look can communicate control. Conversely, we can 'leak' our true feelings of nervousness with a quick twitch or harried movement. In this context, every one of our behaviour management moves can prove crucial.

The first move: Set the behaviour bar high

We can do this by making explicitly clear what good behaviour looks like, sounds like and feels like. Take a moment to ponder that point. It may sound simple and plain common sense, but we too often underestimate the value in doing so, explicitly and repeatedly.

Too many students simply don't know what good learning or good behaviour actually is, and we can too easily overlook this plain truth.

One strategy I have employed with my younger classes with success is to co-create with them a character that embodies the ideal student at the very beginning of the school year. At first it only cues a series of simplistic stereotypes, but when you get students to unpick the specific behaviours of such a student – how they ask questions; how they work in group situations; their physical behaviour when they are listening, etc – it builds up a picture of the behaviours you expect in a usefully concrete fashion.

The value is making such desirable behaviours real, embodied in a simple character, so that we can use that as our high bar of expected behaviour. That character can be emblazoned on the classroom wall as a reminder.

Alternatively, we can simply repeat, repeat and repeat our expectations so that good behaviour is explicit and obvious for all. It may take some valuable curriculum time to do it, but time taken to establish parameters of behaviour rarely proves to be lost time.

We know that we, as teachers, can too often suffer from the 'curse of the expert'. That is to say, we can overlook the nuanced behaviours that made us successful learners in our time at school.

Take the seemingly simple act of listening. We need to show students how to listen actively. Students need to understand the language of non-verbal communication: leaning in slightly, nodding, giving eye contact and asking questions for clarification, etc. It is a series of implicit behaviours that we need to make explicit.

Simple, shorthand statements matter for confident and clear behaviour management. With the listening described above, students can know exactly what you mean when you simply state 'active listening everybody'. They become the cornerstone of classroom routines and they curtail misbehaviour and shine a light on the behaviours we want and expect. When students learn how to truly listen the results can be revelatory, but simply explaining how to enact these behaviours we wish to see will not make it so.

Repetition of our message, and some dogged determination, is also required.

If you want great work from students you will need to inspire their trust, but we must also make clear that we expect that they dredge every improvement possible out of what they are doing before they can sit back in the glow of their excellent work. This requires making excellent work visible. Once visible, it takes a relentless pursuit of those standards. If work is unfinished, reject it. If work is hurried and even marginally substandard, then reject it.

No doubt it takes effort and time to establish your expectations (and no little organisation to request work to be repeated), but setting the bar high is essential.

Students play a clever game of making judgements. If your standard is higher than another teacher, then they will work harder for you. If they have multiple homework assignments, then they will do your homework first and with their best effort. Of course, the best of all possible worlds is that *every* teacher in the school is working hard at establishing the same standard of excellence, but we must start with our actions and our high expectations first.

The second move: Establish the rules

We come to the subject of much debate: school and classroom rules. Let's keep this simple. Rules do not crush the humanity and individuality of our students. Instead, they provide clear expectations for learning to thrive for everybody.

If you wish, share a dialogue with your students about which rules are the most significant, but don't for a moment think that having clear, no-nonsense rules is a negative act. Have rules, establish them early, and make them an integral part of lesson routines. I have spent the opening lesson of many a school year slowly going through the rules of my classroom.

Every week, these clear and concise messages – three or four should do it – are reiterated and made visible through explanation and example.

For me, respect and listening to others is paramount, as I have already stated. Learning flows from the spring of listening. I make respectful and active listening rule number one. I'll often elicit other rules from students, amazing them when my rules nearly exactly match their own. Common rules, like how to move about the classroom and how to respect others, may complete your personal repertoire.

Of course, one lesson does not establish excellent behaviour. That takes habit. I am in favour of a gradual approach. In the first few weeks, consciously note when individual rules are broken, making a not-so-subtle show of following up with sanctions. Sometimes I think most students are in on this charade, but it makes for a feeling of safety and certainty all the same.

By getting organised and establishing consistency in the first few months with our new classes, then we no doubt gain time and improve learning later on in the school year.[3]

The third move: Confidently manage the physical space of the room

Our behaviour management and our teaching begins before the lesson, given our reputation, but even that can be forgotten in the threshing waves of any given day for some of our students. They act on impulses that are too often beyond their conscious control.

Movement and tactical positioning around the classroom space becomes key in initiating your confident control, reminding the students of your status in the room. This is what is meant by the woolly term *presence*.

The opening of the lesson is clearly a crucial point for establishing your control. We can enact a series of small behaviours that convey assertiveness: greeting students at the door of the room with a relaxed smile, conveying preparedness and calm, primes your students for positive behaviour. Fumbling at the computer and searching frantically for your lesson resource sends the wrong message to your class.

The welcome into the classroom also allows you to make those crucial judgements about the mood of your students, settling and reassuring those students who need it. As we know, expert teachers know their students well and read their smallest of behaviours, responding flexibly when required.

Once they are in the classroom you can take up a central space in the room, conveying the confident call of 'this is my turf!' before then directing students to little jobs, quickly, with short, confident explanations:

- 'John – lined paper, one piece each – thanks.'
- 'Claire, can you lower the blinds a little.'
- 'Boys – bags. Move them under the desk – thank you.'

Too often we use conditional language: 'Could you please hand out the paper John?' or 'Would you mind listening please?' Although polite, using a tentative question, rather than a command, sends a small but significant message to our students that they could refuse your direction. You needn't forsake politeness: saying thank you can be positive without losing the power and clarity of a command. We can prove respectful, whilst making students subconsciously assume the behaviour you have directed is quite natural and appropriate.

We should err on the side of using commands and steer clear from tentative requests. If we couple our assertive commands with decisive gestures: pointing toward the paper tray, tapping on the bags to be moved, and more, we will then strike students as confident and authoritative. Once their confidence in us is established, we can choose to gradually ease off with our assertiveness.

Anticipating small acts of off-task behaviour, like chatting absent-mindedly, or talking whilst another student is giving an explanation, can often demand an all-seeing eye. We cannot hope for the head movement of an owl, so regularly moving around the room, anticipating and modifying how students behave, is essential. It can be done quietly and subtly if you position yourself in the eye-line of students, with a little nimble movement about the room.

A phantom pen tapper, or a hellish whistling pen, has foxed most teachers at one time or another. Listening intently, we can scan the class for clues of the furtive act. We shouldn't berate the class en masse. Instead, we can confidently manage our space. First, we move in the direction of the sound. We wait patiently. If we gain control and silence we can move on, but if the sound reappears, we can subtly speak to a narrow group of suspected students, warning them of repercussions and, if absolutely necessary, undertake a lengthy process to establish the root of the problem. If you have high standards and you are relentlessly consistent with them, they will invariably back down.

Expert teachers cut off the oxygen of misbehaviour at the source by managing the space in the room. They spy some stray eye contact when students should be working and they clench a furrowed brow to indicate their subtle command to refocus. For a student tapping away or humming a tune, the universal gesture of a finger pressed to the lips proves an unobtrusive and clear signal of confident control.

Expert teachers control the classroom space, creating their own consistent paths around the room. In his book, *Teach Like A Champion*, which is filled with useful tips for behaviour management, Doug Lemov suggests that teachers should have the confidence to 'break the plane'. That is to say, moving beyond that imaginary line a few feet from the front of the classroom, usually just in front of the first desks where the students sit to face the teacher. Too many teachers are pinned to the board at the front and others unwittingly retreat to the safe confines behind the teacher desk.

A crucial signal of physical confidence is passing that imaginary boundary to assert our physical influence.

Students quickly become used to your typical positional 'hotspots' around the room and they can commit to being more focused in the knowledge that you are constantly surveying how each student is doing.

A confident teacher's 'presence' can be distilled down to a series of such movements, small signals and gestures. I have experienced a remarkable range of gestures and signals, all understood by students through repeated practice, such as:

- Two hands held horizontally at chest height, lowered slowly [Instruction: lower the volume]
- An arm raised straight in the air [Instruction: be silent]
- Raised eyebrows [Instruction: think about your current behaviour!]

To convey confidence and presence, waving frantically like a distressed air traffic controller isn't going to cut it. We must emit calm and control when directing behaviour. When we convey physical equanimity, our students subconsciously feel safer and their behaviours can become more controlled. Being a teenager is a risky business and their brains are built for unthinking, boundary-shoving behaviour, but we can becalm them and set them more at ease.

The fourth move: Voice control

Expert behaviour management can prove near hidden – a silent treatment where students can continue to focus intently on what is being learnt. There are of course many occasions when you need to quell misbehaviour by speaking assertively.

Simple and clear commands are the order of the day for the confident teacher. Too often, I have suffered in silence when observing a teacher who is desperately shushing their group. Some teachers, visibly lacking in confidence, shush away like a Victorian steam train. Students, given the opportunity, will judge the vague shush in their general direction as not being directed at them. It proves little more than hot air.

Instead, we need to convey a short, sonorous instruction: 'James: quiet – now. Thank you'. When we pare down our language to the essentials like this it is both direct and is less likely to disrupt the flow of the lesson for others.

The tone and expression in our voice is vital in conveying our confidence. A handy reminder is to be frog-like in delivery. Green frogs frighten off potential rivals with a deep croak and, of course, the bigger the frog the deeper the croak. Only wily and small green frogs have learnt to deepen their voice to imitate their bigger peers too. The power of our voice is similarly available to every teacher.

153

We should be wary of judging that such an approach favours only male teachers with a naturally deep voice. Female teachers can exercise the same subtle message to students by deepening their tone compared to their typical voice. It is about making minor, but important, adjustments to our voice that can have a significant impact upon how our words are received.

Teachers, to convey assurance, can gradually lower their volume as they explain – subtly making students listen with extra focus – whilst deepening the tone of voice. Consciously varying and deepening our tone of voice is the stuff of stage actors and expert teachers, but it can be learnt and we can covertly experiment with our students when we get the chance.

Remember Doug Lemov talked about the power of practice. Varying our voice for effect is ripe for such practice.

We each have our unique personal voice, but we should consider that when teaching we are using our 'stage' voice – our *act-of-utter-confidence* voice. Our teaching voice has greater range, more emotion, and it conveys more explicit emphasis than our 'normal' voice. I have been caught once or twice using my 'teacher voice' when annoyed with my partner. Though it clearly didn't work with her – perhaps the fact that she recognised the different tone and range in my voice is no bad thing...or not.

Teach Like a Champion once again proves instructive. It is important that whilst we expect to control our voice, lowering our volume and deepening our tone when appropriate, we need the full attention of every student. Lemov simplifies this down to the hook: *100 per cent.*

It is simple. Always expect one hundred per cent attention. If we ask for silence, to listen to a student give a response, we need one hundred per cent active listening. It is common sense personified, but sometimes common sense isn't so common.

Any allowance for a lesser standard of behaviour and students will commit it to memory (and not in a good way). To allow students to chat to others when a fellow student is speaking is for me a cardinal sin. If '100 per cent' is not established here, then we will be unlikely to establish the classroom climate where great learning happens.

Allowing a lowly murmur of chatter will wholly undermine your authority and lower expectations. When we are tired, our willpower strained by a hard week, the temptation is to marginally loosen our expectations. We can easily slump in our chairs, letting minor rule-breaking go. We must fight off this quite natural urge.

If our classroom rules and expectations are well honed, we can loosen control with comfort, but our safest judgement is to always retain one hundred per cent consistency.

The fifth move: Managing confrontation

A student who is out of control is the stuff of sleepless nights for teachers. No aspect of teaching can generate the degree of worry that out of control student behaviour creates. We need to act with assertive confidence when such an incident occurs.

I have faced this type of situation many times and have always attempted to best judge the situation with care and sensitivity.

I started this chapter with the story of Jessica. Too many times she approached my classroom visibly ready to explode. A split second judgement was required. Our face is the prime communicator of our emotion. Her face told a bleak story. Entering the classroom or not was a key decision. Would not paying attention help to disarm the anger, or did Jessica need time outside of the classroom to cool off? What do you do?

Given such a crisis, a series of physical responses are required to help diffuse the emotions of the angry child:

- **Recognise our stress.** The natural reaction is to match the strain of our angry student with a defensive raising of our voice to be heard, or by naturally assuming a defensive posture, such as halting students by pointing directly at them. We must fight this physical urge and concentrate on speaking slowly, calmly, in an assured voice.
- **Assume a non-threatening body position.** First, we need to take care not to threaten the student by conveying aggression. We can assume a non-threatening stance, such as standing sideways and avoiding a direct face-to-face position.
- **Take care with eye contact.** Where eye contact typically establishes a relationship, in such an instance of anger and loss of control, taking care to look away and not stare can help.
- **Mirroring and calm gestures.** The minutiae of our body language is essential. Avoid pointing or clenched fists – signs of stress and challenge – and instead place your arms by your side, using open hand gestures if needed. A subtle mirroring of their body language can help ease their anxiety and diffuse potential confrontation.
- **Listen.** When a student is angry, unsurprisingly, they can find it hard to think rationally. We need to take care to verbalise that we are listening. Calmly replying, 'I understand what you mean', or paraphrasing what they are exclaiming in clearer terms, can show that you are ready and willing to listen. Often, we need to let students articulate their anger, but it does need guidance.
- **Identify and explain the problem.** Once we are talking to the student and they are offloading, we can assert our confident control by appraising the problem and explaining it to them clearly.
- **Assert our position with calm.** We need to explain how we feel about their behaviour, about the lesson ahead, and the other students who need our attention.

156

We can acknowledge what we want and what we don't want, before recognising their response.

● **Negotiate with care.** We can never concede ground that means our other students may have their learning compromised, but listening and negotiating the best settlement to see a solution ahead is required. The teen brain is programmed to revel in risk and not to consider the consequences. Sometimes a little time is all that is required, but at other times, calmly articulating and applying the familiar school sanctions proves essential.

Instances of erupting anger and discord are commonplace even in the best schools. They can be diffused or exacerbated in a matter of seconds. We can take a leaf out of the book of a doctor in this instance. A typical conversation with a patient, which can of course prove intensely private and distressing, can be just like an incident in school with a highly emotional student, so we can take care to deploy the *BATHE technique.* This applies to the approach we take to our interaction:

Background ('Tell me about what has happened in the lesson.')

Affect ('How do you feel about what happened and what was said?')

Trouble ('What is upsetting you most about what was said in the lesson?')

Handling ('How are you feeling about what X said to you in the lesson?')

Empathy ('That must have been really difficult for you...')

Such an event in the school day, showing empathy and soothing a distressed student, can prove our most important action. We need to approach it with a calm confidence.

Great group work

Group work is often conflated with poor student behaviour. Perhaps this is understandable given that, done badly, group work can prove a hotbed for misbehaviour. Conversely, done well, and given a tight structure, with clarity of roles and expectations, group work can prove a highly useful tool in the classroom.

The benefits of group talk are legion. They are shown in the development of crucial social skills, like empathy and seeing the viewpoints of others, accommodating them and developing our thinking. Well orchestrated, the knowledge of a group can outdo that of an individual, as the group aggregates and sifts through an array of ideas.

Opportunities for misbehaviour are naturally ingrained in the DNA of group work that is not well managed. 'Social loafing' is an all too common occurrence. When students are placed in a group they can take the opportunity to exert less effort, grabbing the chance to loaf, knowing their peers will make up for their slacking. Teachers can subsequently reward students unfairly, given one or more of the group have done all the work, whilst others were happy to coast along effortlessly.

Group work, quite naturally, can devolve into off-task chatter and impromptu social bonding on any topic that catches our students' interest. The benefits of cooperative small group work are too often outweighed by teachers lacking the confidence and skill to control and manage this learning method.

Indeed, such small group work is used relatively sparingly, with a recent study indicating less than 10 per cent of lesson time was spent doing group work.[4]

We should aim for a position where we are confident to deploy the right teaching strategy at the right time and not seeking to avoid any one approach for fear of it failing.

Thorough-going preparation for group work is a prerequisite for success and there are some sound principles for successful group work:

- **Establish the ground rules.** Once more, ensuring what we mean by communication – talk, listening, sharing and participating, etc – needs to be made visible to students, regardless of their age and stage. The few minutes invested in asking questions like, 'What do I mean by good collaboration?' are quickly regained when focused group discussion doesn't quickly dissolve into a meaningless debate about the best Marvel superhero.
- **Clear roles and goals.** Establishing clear roles, like researcher, summariser, note-taker, etc, all encourage focused discussion and learning, dissuading the temptation to loaf. What is really crucial is that there are group goals, but with individual responsibility.[5] One method is to have a group goal, such as producing code for a new school website in a computing class. Within that group goal though, there would be individual responsibilities that require each student to transfer important knowledge to one another, making them responsible for a distinct aspect of the task. By ensuring this reliance on one another, you can better eliminate loafing, thereby fairly balancing the workload in the group.
- **Precision timing.** We know we can all be downright awful at judging how long a task will take. For novice teachers, this is especially so. To ensure that behaviour is focused on the task, we need to share a dialogue about timing, giving markers along the way, without proving to be too much of a distraction.
- **Short, sharp stops.** Chatting and off-task behaviour is usually a product of waning interest and a lack of focus. It can happen with the most interesting of tasks, no

matter how well designed. It is important to judge the flow of the group working and stop at regular intervals. My experience indicates that students need refocusing (with an option for questions) every ten to fifteen minutes or so.

● **Monitoring.** Owning the classroom space and tactical positioning about the room throughout group work is essential. A confident teacher will recognise the subtle signs of loafing or chatting, before quickly asking short prompt questions, like, 'How are we progressing?' just to remind students of their role and responsibility. Sometimes groups will reach a genuine impasse that requires support. We must avoid learned helplessness, so asking them to reiterate the problem and talk through potential solutions, with short prompts, is a must.

With each group task we should be keenly aware of the subtle group dynamics at play. We know that the teen brain is thirsty to belong in their social group, so students often look to their important peers for validation and even consent. Each class has some 'key players' who set the tone in such group tasks. We must have a sharp understanding of the hierarchy at play here and form the groups accordingly.

There is no doubt that our degree of confidence in leading the class and managing such scenarios sends explicit messages to those 'key players' who are in control of the group dynamics, which are subtly shared between students.

Keeping in the flow

As explored earlier in the book, the notion of 'flow', made popular by Mihaly Csikszentmihalyi, describes a state of near complete immersion in a task. It captures that feeling when you are quite literally loving learning: you are getting useful feedback and you are finding your way. It might be best captured in that treasured moment when your student says, 'Is the lesson over already? That was quick!' Indeed, time seems to fly when you are in full 'flow'.

Confident behaviour management is about creating the conditions for this 'flow' to happen. It requires challenging work that pushes students without seeing them flailing; it takes timely feedback and a sensitive observation of the learning in the room; it takes trust in the teacher for our students to let go of their psychological barriers and anxieties, so that they can get stuck into challenging tasks.

This 'flow' is so crucial because it correlates with students maximising their time on task. By creating routine behaviours to maintain 'flow', we achieve a thousand marginal gains of time throughout the school year. Therefore a teacher with excellent behaviour management is more likely to see significant improvements in students' learning over the longer term.

Teachers know it when we see it, but it pays for us to talk about it and to best characterise what it looks like and sounds like in our own school context.

Take a moment to consider the last time you had a class in full flow. What was the activity and what were the strategies that you used to maintain such learning? If we can break it down into a pattern of moves, then we can seek to replicate it more often.

Seeing our students rise to the challenge and exhibit passion and pride in their work is what forges good relationships and great learning. It is what we go to school for. We can see, feel and feed off such responses from even the most challenging of students. That feeling we experience can in turn deepen our sense of commitment and hope, and it can sustain our confidence.

IN SHORT...

- We know that thinking and feeling are bound together to form our behaviours. Knowing our students and developing a trusting relationship is paramount for us to become truly confident in our behaviour management skills.

- A classroom climate characterised by focus and high effort is synonymous with successful learning. It requires clear and consistent parameters of behaviour being established. If a student is late, we relentlessly deal with that lateness; if there is a school-wide behaviour policy, we follow that policy with rigour (if there isn't, then we pursue our own as best we can).

- There are behaviour hotspots: the starts of lessons, transitions between tasks, and the ends of lessons are where misbehaviour most commonly flourishes. We need to take physical control of the classroom space at all times, but particularly at these points in our lessons.

- Expert behaviour management can appear somewhat invisible, but momentary gestures and shorthand instructions can characterise clarity, consistency and control.

- Confident teachers sweat the small stuff so that big behaviour incidents almost never develop. It looks quick and easy, but it takes a great deal of effort and expertise.

- We know that our confidence to manage poor behaviour and challenging classes is paramount for our students' success and for our well-being as teachers.

Notes

1 Kidd, C., Palmeri, H. and Aslin, R.N. (2013), 'Rational snacking: Young children's decision-making on the marshmallow task is moderated by beliefs about environmental reliability', *Cognition* 126: 109–114. [Online]. Available at: www.bcs.rochester.edu/people/aslin/pdfs/ Kidd_Palmeri_Aslin_Cog2013.pdf (Accessed: 5 January 2015).

2 Zimmerman, B.J. (2000), 'Self-efficacy: An essential motive to learn', *Contemporary Educational Psychology*, 25: 82–91.

3 Cameron, C.E, McDonald Connor, C. and Morrison, F.J. (2005), 'Effects of variation in teacher organization on classroom functioning', *Journal of School Psychology*, 43 (1): 61–85.

4 Muijs, D. and Reynolds, D. (2011) *Effective Teaching: Evidence and Practice (3rd Edition)*, p 65. London: Sage Publications.

5 Slavin, R.E. (1995), *Co-operative Learning: Theory, Research and Practice (2nd Edition)*, Boston: Allyn and Bacon.

Section 3
Confident pedagogy

10 Some core principles for teaching and learning

It is easy to bewail the negative impact politicians the world over can have on our education system. Yet, despite all the standardised national tests and attempts by policymakers, and even school leaders, to standardise practice in the classroom, the real truth is that the teacher conducts the vast majority of what goes on in the classroom in splendid isolation.

The teacher is still, despite all, in charge. For this reason, no 'improvement' is done unto us or without our consent.

A curriculum can and will shift, and we will be guided to teach in certain ways according to changing fashions, but our actions will predominantly remain our own when we close the door and teach. Sometimes we will be under scrutiny, but a mere spell of being observed conveys little about who we are or what we do in the classroom each day.

We can bemoan the ill-judged treatment of teachers, which we should articulate with a collective voice, yet we can still focus on our self-improvement and develop our own knowledge and confidence in our classroom.

We know teaching to be an ancient practice with the richest of traditions. Picture Socrates enrobed in his toga asking tough questions and giving some acerbic feedback. Has teaching changed so much from his central triumvirate of explaining, asking great questions and giving rich feedback? How about we stick a tie on Socrates and perhaps we could fit him out with a room, a computer and a projector. He would likely fit in just fine!

Too many people complicate and rebrand teaching methods, but the core fundamentals of good teaching remain remarkably resistant to fads and the changeable winds of political policy relaunches (or simply rehashes).

We don't need the endless buzzwords or the glossy resources beloved by educational companies selling their people and their wares. The tools and the technology may change, but how we teach and how we learn stays remarkably stable. We can draw confidence when developing our practice by focusing upon these long-practised principles of great teaching.

We can reduce the brilliant complexity of teaching down to this rather simple cycle: we *explain, we question, we model our thinking, we get students to practice and in turn they get feedback on that practice.* We do so repeatedly, each time growing our students' knowledge, seeing it expand and grow like the rings of an oak tree.

Teaching and learning is as simple and as complex as that.

'Expert moves' and best practice

We know that teachers around the world experience many more similarities than differences in their experience of teaching children. Some classrooms are packed with technology and are fortuitously situated in brilliant new building designs, whereas other classrooms can be barely called a room fit for learning.

No matter the setting, learning happens.

Earlier, in Chapter 4, the notion of expertise was explored, alongside the attendant 'moves' of expert teachers. Barak Rosenshine, educational psychologist and researcher from the University of Illinois (and former teacher of US History), has distilled his forty years of studying teacher improvement into what he has described as his 'principles of instruction'. I can find no better description of the moves of an expert teacher:

- *Begin a lesson with a short review of previous learning.*
- *Present new material in small steps with student practice after each step.*
- *Limit the amount of material students receive at one time.*
- *Give clear and detailed instructions and explanations.*
- *Ask a large number of questions and check for understanding.*
- *Provide a high level of active practice for all students.*
- *Guide students as they begin to practice.*
- *Think aloud and model steps.*
- *Provide models of worked-out problems.*
- *Ask students to explain what they have learned.*
- *Check the responses from all students.*
- *Provide systematic feedback and corrections.*
- *Use more time to provide explanations.*
- *Provide many examples.*

Some core principles for teaching and learning

- *Reteach material when necessary.*
- *Prepare students when they begin independent practice.*[1]

So here is our checklist – we can now all go home and rest easy.

Of course, there are a few problems with this seemingly simple solution. First, we are likely to suffer from what Professor Rob Coe calls the 'motherhood and apple pie'[2] problem. Like 'motherhood and apple pie', we can all agree with Rosenshine's principles; yet, we too easily agree, assuming that we do all of these things, so these principles become everything to all people, actually resulting in few of us faithfully enacting them at all.

We follow these principles, right?

Only, what do we mean by practice? What is a clear and detailed explanation?

If we are to become truly confident teachers then we should dig beneath the surface of the checklist and immerse ourselves in the evidence that purports to describe great teaching, before then applying it with good judgement to our classroom context. We can then combine such evidence with our craft knowledge and our unique understanding of our own students. Such knowledge combined creates a sort of alchemy where learning happens – with this knowledge and understanding we can grow our confidence in our practice in the classroom.

So what best practice do we need to know?

Being a confident teacher means that excellent knowledge of our particular subject, or subjects, is essential. Yet, crucially, being a confident mathematician does not make you a great teacher of mathematics. If it did, we could simply filter out teaching candidates by their university degree class and be done with it. We know that this isn't the case in reality.

Teaching no doubt requires deep subject knowledge, but great learning relies upon the unique alchemy of the teacher/student relationship. Wedded to this, we need to understand *how* students best learn that subject. Expert teachers work hard at adapting the materials at hand, proving they are flexible to the needs of the students in front of them, ceaselessly making subtle judgements and asking important questions, such as:

- What prior knowledge do my students possess?
- What are the best analogies to help explain a topic?
- What are the common misconceptions for this topic?
- What methods best erase those misconceptions?
- What questions will prove their understanding and elicit deeper learning?

Shulman puts it nicely when he reverses the ignorant nonsense about teachers are those that cannot 'do', with his sage aphorism, quoting Aristotle, that 'those who can, do; those who understand, teach'. It takes a great deal of understanding to marry subject knowledge, the knowledge of how to communicate it, with a refined grasp of how students learn it.

In reality, there is a lot that we need to *understand* before we can achieve the degree of confidence exemplified by the teacher expert.

More than just subject knowledge

For a teacher of mathematics, being an expert mathematician is no doubt important. Strong content knowledge for all teachers at every phase is powerful. It can help free up a teacher to respond and to 'seize teachable moments'.[3] That is to say, if they can spot hurdles in understanding, they can fill in gaps of knowledge with a perceptive understanding of the subject content.

When I notice that my students are struggling to grasp the concept of a metaphor in my English class, then my capacity to use a range of examples and provide additional explanations with assurance can seize the 'teachable moment'. When Rosenshine describes great teachers breaking new material into small steps, there is a requirement to deeply grasp the material to be able to break it down and piece it back together appropriately.

Confident subject knowledge frees up a teacher to concentrate upon how the students are learning, and this has a lot of value. Crucially, however, it isn't the singular factor in making a confident teacher. It is not enough. Indeed, once you reach a certain degree of subject knowledge expertise, beyond what the students are required to know, the returns in the classroom begin to diminish.

There is a more important factor, a more subtle knowledge, which is a combination of knowing the content matter, the students, and a wide range of teaching strategies. Shulman called this 'subject pedagogical knowledge', or SPK for short. SPK goes further and deeper than a university degree and it best describes the confident teacher expert.

Take a moment: a scientific *moment*.

Now, the scientists and physicists among us would instantly recognise the meaning of the word 'moment'. They would give you an assured definition – 'the moment of a force is a measure of its tendency to cause a body to rotate about a specific point or axis'. For most of us – that isn't the first thought in our minds when we hear the word 'moment'.

Clearly, confident teaching requires such subject expertise. It would also necessitate some excellent SPK to best translate this scientific concept to many students. This would start with a skilled, clear explanation, before going on to deepen their understanding.

Our pedagogical knowledge is tested: what demonstrations would work best to exemplify a 'moment'? Would you begin with the most common analogy of a see-saw to describe the concept?

An expert teacher may use multiple analogies and they may get two students to demonstrate a 'moment' (if both students were opposite sides of the classroom door, pushing with equal force they would create equilibrium – if one student stopped pushing, the student still pushing would create a 'moment').

You can see SPK consistently on display in the classroom of an expert: the right selection of a task; the choice of explanation with just the right analogy to hook into the fertile minds of the group; the deft coordination of discussion and the teasing questions that elicit understanding – with just the right degree of feedback, at just the right time. Of course, getting it 'just right' is a tricky endeavour.

With a deep knowledge of both our subject knowledge and SPK, whilst harnessing a confident grasp of the fundamental 'moves' of great teaching: explanations, questioning and feedback, modelling and metacognition, we free ourselves to then try out innovations in our practice with greater assurance.

The Pareto Principle

There exists a dizzying array of teaching strategies for us to choose from. The numbers of tools available, particularly when harnessing new technologies, is quite simply vast. If I were to write a book about all of these strategies and tools it would sink a boat. Instead, the aim of this section is to focus upon the *valuable few* that we can be confident have the greatest impact.

Some core principles for teaching and learning

The 'Pareto Principle', otherwise known as 'the law of the valuable few', is simple. It proffers that roughly 80 per cent of an effect comes from 20 per cent of the causes. Applied to our teaching: 80 per cent of our success with students comes from a core 20 per cent of our teaching strategies.

What is the secret of the 20 per cent you rightly ask? Well, I don't offer any guarantees here, but for me, common sense dictates that becoming confident at some of the strategies that we use most commonly, on a daily basis, would bring us nearer the secret of the 20 per cent.

The six strategies I offer as being the crucial few are **explanations, questioning** and **feedback, modelling** and **metacognition** (that is to say, getting students to think hard about their thinking) and **memory for learning**.

Take that in for a moment. When did you last carefully devise an explanation you were about to give? When was the last time that you took the time to compose a powerful sequence of questions before a lesson?

These fundamental facets of what we do, the glue that binds together teaching and learning, are to be found within these valuable few. Too often, though, our focus and time are subsumed in creating glossy resources and designing elaborate activities, or filling in bureaucratic necessities in lesson pro formas. The fundamental processes I have outlined, evident in Rosenshine's excellent evidence-based 'principles of instruction', can too easily be ignored and replaced with shinier alternatives.

Happily, a focus on these valuable few learning strategies has significant implications for our workload. If we concentrate upon these few strategies, with an acute observance of the language we use and the effort we can inspire from our students, then we can outdo any attempt to slave over elaborate resources, the cooking up of vast projects, or even the putting on of energy-draining extra teaching sessions.

Our self-improvement can be both manageable and sustainable. By surveying the best evidence, developed over decades by researchers and teachers alike, we can be more confident that, by careful application, we can make significant improvements to our teaching practice.

A caution against overconfidence

We have explored already that overconfidence can make people deaf to advice and can be wholly damaging to any professional – from the classroom to the boardroom.

Remember the mental biases back in Chapter 3? We seek to confirm our beliefs about what works in the classroom and this is invariably rooted in our past experience. If we have tried a teaching strategy before then we stick with it, and if someone challenges our practice then we invariably fight our corner.

If we are planning together in groups, we will defer to the loudest and most confident voice in the group, who in turn will likely be basing their decisions upon their own limited knowledge. We can fend off this 'group think' by widening our net of knowledge when it comes to teaching strategies.

Now, you may be forgiven for thinking that I am bringing the experience, wisdom and intuition of teachers into question here. I am not. We should put a great deal of stake in the value of experience and our 'craft knowledge'; and yet, we should test and challenge our teaching experience with other sources of evidence. It could be a teacher coach, a critical friend, or the reading of books, blogs and websites on teaching and learning.

Being more critical and less confident in what we have done habitually in the past can prove beneficial to our attempt to improve our practice.

We should be open to different strategies and approach our practice with an open mind and deep-seated humility.

If we closely track the impact of our practice, with disciplined trial and error, then we can better evaluate what we do in the classroom.

Teachers are typically time poor so such self-evaluation can prove both difficult and time-consuming, but a little short-term pain may lead to our long-term gain.

Remember, a confident teacher is an expert who knows the limits of their expertise, whilst always retaining the belief that they can improve and develop.

IN SHORT...

- As the wheel of fortune always turns, so go the latest teaching fads and fashions. Fend off the quick fixes and the latest teaching trends, screw your courage to the wheel, and remain true to the time-worn principles of great teaching.
- Barak Rosenshine defines his crucial 'principles of instruction'. Ask yourself, what are your core principles for teaching and learning?
- Whilst we rightly recognise the crucial importance of teacher subject knowledge, we must endeavour to also develop our subject pedagogical knowledge: the communication of our subject knowledge to our students.
- As we busily attempt to seize those 'teachable moments' in the classroom, we should concentrate on honing the valuable few moves of the confident teacher expert.

Notes

1   Rosenshine, B. (2010), 'Principles of instruction', UNESCO Educational Practices Series – 21, International Bureau of Education.

2   Coe, R. (1999), 'Manifesto for evidence-based education', [Online]. Available at: www.cem.org/attachments/ebe/manifesto-for-ebe.pdf (Accessed: 30 March, 2015).

3   Kahan, J.A., Cooper, D.A. and Bethea, K.A. (2013), 'The role of mathematics teachers' content knowledge in their teaching: A framework for research applied to a study of student teachers', *Journal of Mathematics Teacher Education*, 6 (3): 223–252.

11 Exemplary explanations

Recapitulations, illustrations, examples, novelty of order, and ruptures of routine – all these are means for keeping the attention alive and contributing a little interest to a dull subject. Above all, the teacher must be alive and ready, and must use the contagion of his own example.

William James, *Talks to Teachers: On Psychology and to Students on Some of Life's Ideals*

Consider a conservative estimation of how long we spend each day giving explanations in the classroom. Then think about how much planning time we give over to those very same explanations. The typical answer is very little.

Back in 1892, before a thousand books about teaching emerged, William James, the famous psychologist and brother to the novelist Henry James, spoke to teachers 'On Psychology: And to Students on Some of Life's Ideals'. He made some thoroughly modern insights into teaching and learning that cognitive science has since corroborated.

He analysed the minutiae of giving memorable explanations and the voluntary, and the often involuntary, attention of our students. The act of explaining is not as simple as handing over the baton of knowledge. The attention of our students is influenced by an array of factors, including the trust and interest each student invests in their teacher, the actions of their friends, the limits of their vocabulary and working memory, and so much more.

Seeking out something like a pattern for memorable explanations may appear somewhat of a fool's errand – a pinning the tail on the donkey affair. Still, we can make some good approximations about what may stick best that can instil confidence in our attempt to deliver great explanations.

Connect to what they know

Perhaps the most important starting point for any teacher when considering what and how to teach is to first find out what students already know. It seems so obvious and easy, but this is no simple venture.

Graham Nuthall, a New Zealand researcher, filmed hundreds of hours of students learning in the classroom for his great book, *The Hidden Lives of Learners*. His findings revealed the chastening truth that most students already know an estimated 50 per cent of the information they are taught. The problem here is that each student knows a different fifty per cent!

What hope is there for us to make sense of this? Each student inhabits his or her own private world of knowledge, skill and understanding: Jake knows the half of it, but Janine is clueless; Alice grasps another aspect, but Alan is none the wiser.

As Barak Rosenshine recommends, we should break down new information so that it doesn't overwhelm our students' capacity to remember, using lots of examples and helping our students undertake purposeful practice. He identifies that the most effective teachers spend double the time in explaining, giving examples, demonstrating and asking questions, than the least effective teachers. This means more explanations and careful judgement too.

By giving a series of examples we can better hope to pin the tail of new learning onto their prior knowledge.

We therefore need to ensure that our explanations are long enough to hook onto the prior knowledge of our students, but not overly long so that they are faced with a confusing mass of information. There is the common-sense notion, supported by what researchers describe as the 'the expertise reversal effect'[1], that if we give too much information to our students, then they are likely going to struggle to remember it.

Why is the wealth of background knowledge so important? We learn best by making connections to what we already know. Also, our students draw confidence when they can relate this new idea or concept to what they already know.

Let's take a random Internet headline, by way of example, like this from the Smithsonian website:

'To be or not to be Shakespeare'.[2]

This headline pun requires some substantial knowledge to make it vaguely interesting. First, the reference to Hamlet's soliloquy is drawing upon a cultural knowledge of the famous play. Then the witty addition of Shakespeare himself draws upon the knowledge that Shakespeare's plays have long-since drawn questions regarding their 'true' authorship. Furthermore, knowledge of grammatical rules is important, as a simple comma could change the entire meaning of the headline.

All this knowledge is required to grasp a seven-word headline with a mildly witty pun. The article hasn't even begun to test the limits of the prior knowledge of our students.

In the face of the complexity our students face, too often teachers suffer from what can be termed as the 'curse of the expert' (once more, it indicates the dangers of overconfidence when we are making judgements). We assume our students have much of the tacit cultural knowledge that we take for granted. As a teacher of literature, I may easily, but falsely given my overconfidence, assume that Hamlet's famous line is commonly known amongst all my students.

To overcome this 'curse' we can elaborate on the example, giving us the opportunity to explain further and to eliminate misconceptions and plug gaps in their knowledge.

First, we can ask them if they understand the pun and the famous reference. Second, we can reinforce our explanation of a pun, to check everyone shares the same understanding. Then we can make connections to examples they know well, perhaps from their prior school experience, or from their shared popular interests. Finally, we can devise an example with them, before getting them to do so, in pairs or individually, using the model of another exemplar to give them a start, such as:

'Who was Shakespeare?' That is (still) the question.' *The Guardian.*[3]

By packing our explanations full of clear and effective examples we can, over time, help our students better connect their learning. Like expert teachers, we can then encourage students to create a web of connections in their mind, synchronising their knowledge into schemas.

Exemplary explanations

We need to help them build their prior knowledge (often it is also a case of developing their vocabulary) more explicitly and systematically. We should be wary that our expert 'teacher language' can all too easily obscure our meaning for our novice students, when what is required is to make our explanations clear at every step.

Useful teaching strategies to trigger prior knowledge for learning:

- **The best example?** Give a sequence of examples in your explanation to exemplify an idea or concept. Students can then select what they deem the most helpful or representative example and explain why.
- **Twenty questions.** Get students to ask 'twenty questions' about a topic before they study it. The complexity and range of their questions will go a long way to helping you frame what they know and then what they need to know, whilst also giving you reference points for your explanation.
- **Pre-quizzing.** Ascertain their prior knowledge by setting them a quiz *before* you even explain a topic, rather than just at the end of a topic.
- **Think-pair-share.** Get students to 'think-pair-share' about the topic at hand before or after an explanation. Have them talk about the explanation, share their ideas/ views, and then share back in whole group feedback. This offers us the opportunity to elicit useful feedback and to solve misconceptions.
- **What is in a word?** Explicitly teach the etymology of subject-specific terms, connecting them to common families of words.

Tell the story

In his excellent book, entitled, *Why Don't Students Like School?* Daniel Willingham made the perceptive insight that stories are 'psychologically privileged' for our students and us.

He gets to the root of all great explanations: the telling of a memorable story. Stories are contagious and personal stories even more so.

Take a minute and try to recall some of your more memorable teachers. Do you remember their personal stories all these years later?

When it comes to explaining tricky concepts, the telling of stories can aid understanding like few other strategies. If I recall my school experience once more, I can remember little of chemistry lessons, but I can recite much of the emotionally charged biography of Marie Curie.

As a father, I am pretty sure that much of the detailed knowledge of ancient Egypt understood by my daughter is sparked by her interest in the famous story of Cleopatra. Any effective explanation must cultivate such curiosity and draw upon the power of such narratives.

Consider what you have already read of this book. I would imagine that some of the personal stories have proven most memorable to you. Pick out three elements of the book that have proved memorable so far. Ask yourself: were any of these personal stories?

Research has shown that bringing history, science and more to life with stories can prove memorable. One such study compared students reading a text about using Galileo's telescope with a typical explanation (expository writing) with the same information in a narrative style, with Galileo as a character. One week later, the narrative version proved far more memorable for students.[4]

Exemplary explanations

Experienced teachers deploy this tactic all the time in their explanations, bringing their subject figuratively alive.

When a teacher reveals a little of their life to their students it can prove strikingly memorable to students too – more so than we might expect.

To many students teachers are simply not quite human! Seeing them in the street, just walking and talking, can prove an epiphany for some. When we reveal we are real people, with real lives just like them, it can provide an initial shock, but then quickly they are better able to trust and believe our explanations and our stories tend to stick.

Some teachers baulk at relating anything about themselves to their students, but we can do this within reason and our students gain a great deal from it. Indeed, without establishing a personal and trusting relationship, our artfully crafted explanations will simply not prove as memorable.

Just remember, have a core message that your story illuminates, otherwise you are in danger of making students think about your brilliant story and forgetting the connection to your main idea.

Useful teaching strategies to harness the power of stories:

- **The memory palace.** This ancient memory strategy takes a sequence of objects – each representing a fact or piece of information – and transforms them into a visual story in the setting of a home or 'palace'. If it works for Sherlock Holmes...
- **The biography boost.** Scour your subject for personal stories. If we want to drive home an abstract and complex concept we can find stories to exemplify the idea. For example, if we wanted to convey the powerful plasticity of the human brain in a biology lesson, we can relate a personal story of a London taxi driver and how

their brain quite literally changes, growing more grey matter, when they learn the routes of 25,000 streets in London.

- **Tell their story.** Get students to tell their own stories that relate to the explanation. If they can accurately relate their stories, they are showing that they understand the concept at a deeper level.
- **Writing stories.** Transform all of your standard explanatory writing with a narrative slant. Essentially, what 'story' are you telling? To shape your explanations use the 'grammar' of a story: a beginning; a middle – with some conflict; and an end. Are you teaching the history of the Russian Revolution? Then tell it as a compelling story. You can do this in every subject, with pretty much any topic.
- **Story hooks.** Leave them asking why. Go one step further than simply evoking the power of stories by leaving them asking questions with an unresolved ending. This forces students to make active inferences and deeply consider the content of the 'story'.

The magic of metaphor

Grab a pen and a piece of paper and take a minute to undertake the following little task:

Write down a few sentences that describe you in a *good* mood. Now, write some sentences that describe you in a *bad* mood.

Do you notice any patterns of language? Do you employ any clichés or common idioms almost despite yourself? Are metaphors springing up in all their linguistic glory?

Crucially, do you notice an *orientation* for each group of descriptions? Were you consistently 'up' when you described your good mood? Were you 'flying high', or 'on cloud nine'? Were you physically 'down' when you were mired in a bad mood, 'dwelling in the depths of depression', or 'stuck in the gutter'?

Alexander Pope, in his epic poem, 'Ulysses', describes the 'easy art' of speech as practised by the mythic hero Ulysses, who couches his poetry in the art of metaphor. It is so common than it can prove near-hidden, but it can help our explanations 'sink into the heart' as Pope so eloquently, and metaphorically, describes.

We should be wary of assuming an understanding of metaphor is the preserve of those teaching literature. It isn't. It is a fundamental part of our language and how we understand, and explain, the world.

In their classic book, *Metaphors We Live By*, George Lakoff and Mark Johnson unpick how the language of metaphor shapes our very understanding of the world. So much so, we often miss and take for granted metaphors in our everyday talk and writing.

The authors start with the example of arguments. Arguments are expressed and understood in terms of *war*. Consider these examples: 'your arguments are indefensible'; 'she was under attack from his barrage of questions'; 'he defended his position'.

Metaphors are so integral to our understanding of the world it is hard to make explicit something that is so common and implicitly embedded in everything we say, read and write. Record any explanation you may give to students and listen back to it. How many metaphors did you use? How many times did you describe something abstract in concrete terms?

Think of the proverb: 'people who live in glass houses shouldn't throw stones'. That concrete description is the ideal shortcut to understanding. In science, white blood cells are memorably depicted at war with foreign invaders. In psychology, Freud would – rather crudely – help us understand our unconscious desires with the Oedipus myth. Metaphors and stories are everywhere – we need only harness their power.

If we consider the importance of metaphor, we skip quickly to using everyday analogies that our students can understand. If we are teaching mathematics, then angles become an exercise in cake cutting or pizza slicing; equations to define a parabola are understood in the looping arc of a basketball shot. I know that my daughter could relate to you with precision her lesson on fractions when she eats pizza.

Similarly, a geography teacher may explain the concept of the layers of the earth with the analogy of a boiled egg (with a bit of preparation, they could bring one along).

Can you think of any metaphors and analogies that you use to powerful effect? Even better, can you devise some new exemplars to help enrich your explanations?

Start with concrete examples, but then, crucially, students need to move from the concrete, relatable examples, to quickly focusing back upon the trickier abstract ideas and concepts, otherwise they will only remember the real example and not be able to apply it effectively. We should be wary of constantly seeking to endlessly 'keep it real' for our students.

A great explanation doesn't necessarily require glossy animations or crazy YouTube videos to be memorable. In fact, research[5] has shown that using still images in explanations can prove more effective than more extended animations. It is a classic case of less is more. The likely reason is that students are forced to actively think more about the image, thereby generating their own thinking, whilst the animation can threaten to overstretch their memory capacity.

We needn't rid our lessons of multimedia, there are a huge number of gems that we can and should access to bolster our explanations, but we can celebrate the use of well-chosen still images to aid our explanations and get students to concentrate on our language.

Useful teaching strategies to make use of metaphor and analogy:

- **Making metaphors.** Get students to select their own metaphor or analogy for an idea or concept.
- **X represents Y.** Get students to choose an object, or objects, in the classroom that can represent a concept and explain their rationale. You would be amazed how imaginative students can be with the contents of their pencil case.
- **Match the metaphor.** This matching involves selecting a range of metaphors and getting students to see which best represents an idea or a concept. The varied debate could elaborate upon lots of interesting related ideas to deepen their understanding. Take the concept of literary analysis: is it peeling an onion, being a detective, or a combination of both: watery-eyed detectives peeling onions.
- **Word association game.** One way of establishing a better understanding of subject-specific vocabulary is to play a quick game of word association. The patterns of ideas and analogies can prove revealing and memorable.
- **Visualise.** Get students to draw a visual representation of ideas or concepts, before then explaining their rationale. When they create patterns and structures to organise their ideas it reinforces their understanding of the content of the explanation.

Students do the explaining

So you know exactly where to pitch your explanation and you have selected a perfectly crafted story with carefully selected analogies. Your job is done with a sure-fire explanation, right? And yet, despite your seeming confidence, only a matter of days later, it is as if the lesson you planned in immaculate detail never happened.

Learning can prove messy and what sticks in our students' memory is sometimes an inadvertent and haphazard affair. We can only do the best with the tools available, such as deploying some artful repetition, then getting students to engage with our explanations to better lodge them in their memory.

A simple truth about all learning is that deliberate repetition is essential for our students to remember. Graham Nuthall, in his brilliant research observing life in the classroom, made the wise approximation that students required repeated exposure to successfully learn new concepts or ideas – with three proving the magic and memorable number. It is a good rule of thumb for our explaining.

We needn't repeat ourselves so obviously, but we can vary our approach, adapting our explanations, invoking new stories and analogies, questions and more, but planning to explain something three times over a spell of time gets us planning with memory in mind.

We need to ensure that we get students to remember our explanations more deeply, getting them to elaborate upon our explanation and doing some hard thinking. When students have to give explanations themselves, their learning is bolstered by the opportunity to be repeatedly exposed to the material and by the *self-explanation effect* (that is to say, they benefit by being forced to organise the material in their own way).

Students teaching one another has long been a staple strategy in the classroom. It is such a powerful technique that even the act of simply telling a student that they will teach one another can help improve how well they think and learn.[6] It can help students to concentrate and better organise their thinking; it just requires some careful planning.

Useful teaching strategies to get students utilising the power of 'self-explanation':

- **Just a minute.** This strategy is a quick and fun approach to distilling the essentials of the material being learnt. Borrowed from a popular radio comedy show, it is as simple as it sounds. Given any topic or argument, students have to speak for one minute, without pausing or repeating themselves. It can be deceptively tricky (and therefore it is very often quick-fire), but it proves very good practice for our students' speaking and listening skills. This strategy can reinforce an explanation and help us decipher their degree of understanding.
- **Topic triptych.** This strategy focuses upon our students organising their thinking about our explanation in a visual way. Given an explanation, students have to devise their own triptych (a painting made up of three sections) comprising three related images. They then have to explain their design selections. This method often draws upon the power of metaphor and symbols, generating memorable cues for their learning.
- **Ten...three...one.** Once more, this strategy is about boiling down the information into a core message, but this time using words. This idea is easy: condense the key idea of the topic or explanation into ten words (this typically takes the form of a sentence). Then three words, and then, finally, one word. Reducing a complex idea, or topic, into a few words really tests their summarisation skills and gets them doing some hard thinking.
- **Chinese whispers.** We all know the game of Chinese whispers. It can provide a fun method for making an

explanation, or a core message, memorable for students. The comedy distortions of the message offer up the opportunity for a humorous hook for your explanation.

- **Explain everything.** Get students to devise a screencast (a video that narrates audio over images of film) for a given topic, or material that has been explained. If you don't have access to any screencasting technology, then there are handy computer and mobile device applications that make it an easy job. Even the task of devising a prospective script can work just as well.

Bringing it all together

We know that explanations are so common in what we do every day, in each lesson, that it may prove most likely that you slip into your usual habits and the guidance from this chapter may not stick. We need to keep it simple if we are to tweak this daily habit.

It is worth bringing together the four areas into one cohesive example of a classroom explanation. Let's take a scenario I am familiar with as an English teacher. As I write this, I am teaching the play *Othello* to a group of sixth-form students. It is crucial that my students understand the villain, Iago, and specifically his role as an archetypal 'malcontent'.

The first move: Connect to what they know

[You could preface the explanation with an image that includes a series of famous villains from literature.]

We have now been introduced in the opening scene to the character of Iago. What role do we think Iago has in the play?

[Students respond with familiar answers like 'villain' or 'antagonist'.]

191

Exemplary explanations

What villains or antagonists do we know from classical drama?

[A brief discussion of examples they know would take place, typically relating to other Shakespearean villains, or examples you provide, but not exclusively so. Answers may then range to films and television if their knowledge is slim.]

The second move: Tell the story

Yes – we'd typically label such a character as a villain. In Jacobean revenge tragedy, the villain took on quite a specific character type, known as the 'malcontent'. Iago is perhaps the most famous malcontent in all of theatre.

First, can we work out what the term 'malcontent' means?

[Students usually respond to exhibit their understanding of the word 'content' and explain what being contented means.]

Ok, so we know what being content is here. Let's tell the story of the word 'malcontent'. Given this is a villainous character, the prefix 'mal' may prove a clue that this character experiences the opposite of being contented. 'Mal' comes from the French, meaning 'bad or ill'. Think how a machine may 'malfunction', or even the word 'malaria' represents a deadly disease.

The backstory of Iago is important here. He is a well-respected soldier, just like Othello, but he is passed over for a job as Othello's number two. You can see how his unhappiness with this may affect his attitude. Not only that, a character called Cassio has been promoted, who Iago sees as slick talking and grossly undeserving. Iago quickly begins to reveal he hates pretty much everyone.

The third move: Using metaphors and analogies to aid understanding

Now, fortunately, there are no malcontents in the room who are angry at the world and everyone in it – or at least I hope that is the case. We could, though, at a stretch, compare the character stereotype of a malcontent with a stroppy teenager. Even I was one once. I wouldn't listen to the advice from my parents or teachers: everything I thought was wrapped up in my own feelings, and I reacted angrily if I was challenged. I may have even slammed a bedroom door or two.

I was no Iago, manipulating people to their tragic demise, but I'm sure, like me, you experienced the powerful emotion of feeling unhappy with everything and everyone at one point in your development as a young teenager.

The fourth move: Get students to explain what they have understood

[This is a natural point to respond to questions, clarify misconceptions and more, before then giving them an explicit opportunity to show their understanding.]

I want to now give you the opportunity to find out a little more about the character archetype of the 'malcontent'. First though, I'd like you to define a 'malcontent' in just ten words.

[I would then go on to deploy the 'Ten...three...one' strategy outlined earlier in the chapter, before agreeing in whole class feedback upon the best definition of a 'malcontent' that we can come up with.]

You could claim that telling stories or using metaphors and analogies is easy given the topic of stories and literature, but the principles of a memorable explanation apply just as well to mathematics, physical education, or whatever subject domain you care to choose.

These four simple steps can prove a simple memory aid for any given explanation and can give you confidence that you are consistently using a range of subtle strategies to make your explanations exemplary.

IN SHORT...

- We know that a memorable explanation is no passive student performance. Students may be sitting still, but their brain is powerfully active, whirring with hard thinking.
- We need to infuse our explanations with the spark and vigour of a performance (if we don't sound interested, then we cannot expect our students to show any interest either).
- Connecting to our students' prior knowledge is essential for our explanations to be understood and to stick.
- Drawing upon the psychological power of stories, metaphors and analogies is simply essential if we are to make our explanations memorable.
- Engaging our students in interpreting our explanations, and making their own explanations, is crucial in helping them achieve a deep understanding of the information at hand.
- Of course, an explanation would not be complete without the most powerful trigger for an active mind: brain-fizzingly good questions. More on that in the following chapter...

Notes

1   Kalyuga, S., Ayres, P., Chandler, P. and Sweller, J. (2003), 'The expertise reversal effect', *Educational Psychologist*, 38 (1): 23–31.
2   Smithsonian: Stewart, D. (2006), 'To be or not to be Shakespeare'. [Online]. *Smithsonian Magazine*. Available at: www.smithsonianmag.com/people-places/to-be-or-not-to-be-shakespeare-127247606/?no-ist (Accessed: June 5 2015).
3   *Guardian*: Thorpe, V. (2007), 'Who was Shakespeare? That is (still) the question', [Online]. *Guardian* website. Available at: www.theguardian.com/uk/2007/sep/09/theatrenews.theatre (Accessed: June 12 2015).
4   Arya, D.J. and Maul, A. (2012), 'The role of the scientific discovery narrative in middle school science education: An experimental study', *Journal of Educational Psychology*, 104: 1022–1032.
5   Mayer, R.E., Hegarty, M., Mayer, S. and Campbell, J. (2005), 'When static media promote active learning: Annotated illustrations versus narrated animations in multimedia instruction', *Journal of Experimental Psychology: Applied*, 11 (4): 256–265.
6   Washington University in St. Louis (2014), 'Expecting to teach enhances learning, recall'. *ScienceDaily*. Available at: www.sciencedaily.com/releases/2014/08/140808163445.htm (Accessed: 8 August 2014).

12 | Confident questioning and feedback

What if we were to do something an estimated 300 to 400 times a day,[1] 70,000 times a year, but then seldom focus on planning and practicing doing it? It sounds mad, but teachers ask a huge number of questions every day, often without an explicit focus on doing it effectively.

There are some simple and profound insights about learning that teachers know and understand. David Ausubel articulated one such insight: 'The most important factor influencing learning is what the learner already knows. Ascertain this and teach him accordingly.'[2]

We'd better start asking our students good questions to find out what they know. It is at once a simple and a complex task.

Our problem, perhaps unsurprisingly, is that we are overconfident that we are highly effective at questioning. Also, particularly for an experienced teacher who has asked hundreds of thousands of questions, it is hard to unpick deep, ingrained habits.

Questioning is so natural – from birth, our curiosity drives us to ask millions of questions – that we do it unthinkingly. It feels so intuitive when on many occasions we can do it very well without explicit thought, instinctively phrasing and pitching a question to one of our students with skill. Crucially, however, the evidence shows that even though questioning accounts for a third of all teaching time (second only to time given over to explanations), 70 per cent of answers take students less than five seconds and, on average, involve a mere three words.[3] Such limited feedback does not indicate expert questioning on our part.

We likely don't ask as many effective questions as we may confidently believe. Effectively, like a doctor in their surgery, we are hunting a diagnosis to understand how healthy our students' knowledge and understanding is so that we can act upon it. Asking better questions may prove 'the most important factor influencing learning', as Ausubel indicates.

Our questions are typically basic and can fail to challenge our students to think hard enough. The majority of our questions prompt a simple recall of facts (often a game of 'guess what answer is in the teacher's head'), alongside procedural questions like 'Where is your book?' We ask so many of these low-order questions that it's easy for it to become our de facto approach.

Our problems don't stop there. Habitually, we ask a mountain of questions but we then fail to give students the requisite time to answer them well. Despite all of our best efforts, the average 'wait time' that students receive to answer a question is a paltry single second.[4] Though the evidence may prove stark, and it is rather obvious that we should give the recommended wait time of circa five seconds or more, it proves remarkably hard to actually do this on a consistent basis.

Try it. Get a student to time and record your rate of questions and the 'wait time' you offer for a couple of lessons.

I have done it myself and realised how little time I gave my students to think hard. It took a great deal of conscious effort to make even the smallest of changes. I had to give myself small cues and strategies to extend the 'wait time' more consciously, like counting to five in my head, or repeating the question for the student. As my personal experience indicates, even a simple act such as giving students adequate 'wait time' can prove a remarkably resistant habit to break.

In our attempts to keep the flow of the lesson and to ensure we have control, keeping the lesson ticking over with quick, easily answered questions makes sense. Questions to maintain attention can prove a handy behaviour control strategy. Our desire to be in control can go too far, however. We can be prone to interrupting students, or feeding them the 'right' answer when they are tripping up or struggling. Even an unconscious physical signal, like the nod of a head, can steal away their hard thinking.

You may be feeling pretty disconsolate by now. Your flawed attempt at the most basic of communication strategies is exposed and you are busy interrupting your students.

Don't be too hard on yourself – we aren't the only ones. Doctors are interrupters too. In conversations with doctors, patients spoke for a mere eighteen seconds before being interrupted. The problem is that doctors, like teachers, may not get to the bottom of the 'problem' if we interrupt.

We can miss vital evidence for our 'diagnosis' of what our students know and understand.

Akin to teachers assuming our wait time is fulsome, doctors can mistakenly assume that they listened more than they talked during office visits.[5] We also overconfidently estimate what our students actually know. Clearly, we are at the root of something very human and typical in our communication. By being conscious of this fact, we can do something about it. We can get better at asking questions and we can improve our listening too.

There is no doubt that part of our role should be encouraging our students to ask great questions. Students initiating their own questions can prove an excellent indicator of their understanding.

We need to ask deeper, open questions that really probe their understanding of the explanation at hand. Simply asking 'When did Martin Luther King die?' in history class has some value, but the deeper follow-up question, 'Why was Martin Luther King's death a turning point in American history and politics?' is much more likely to challenge their thinking and is therefore more likely to burrow down into their long-term memory.

So, in the spirit of asking questions, here are some handy questions about your questioning in the classroom:

- Do you prepare your questions in advance?
- Do you plan for coherent sequences of questions?
- Do you identify critical questions that will most likely diagnose student misconceptions?
- Do you consciously adapt your questions to the skill level of your students (for example, explaining tricky subject-specific language)?
- Do you ask open questions that probe your students' critical thinking (for example, getting them to compare potential solution strategies)?

- Do you provide your students with enough 'wait time' to prepare and plan their response?
- Do all students consistently get involved in classroom discussion?
- Do you encourage your students to ask questions of one another?
- Do you create a culture where *all* students are confident to give responses to questions?

Asking great questions

The key to asking great questions is to know our students. We can once more employ the 'Goldilocks principle' to our questioning approach: *not too easy, not too hard, but just right*, in terms of the degree of difficulty. With good knowledge of our students, we can go about crafting effective questions with greater confidence.

We know that the vast majority of in-class questions are closed questions that elicit instant and often limited responses, whereas we ask fewer open questions.

There is a simple assumption that 'closed questions bad, open questions good'. This isn't the whole truth.

Closed questions are often essential in taking a litmus test response to knowledge. The closed question in an English class, 'What is foreboding?' can easily be then followed by a more challenging open question, such as 'Why does X use foreboding in this passage?' Both question types are valid and necessary to ascertain what the learner already knows. If we leap too quickly to more challenging open questions, then we may miss a basic knowledge gap about the term 'foreboding' that is inhibiting deeper understanding.

Quick, closed questions can have a beneficial impact on behaviour, ensuring that a lot of students have to respond and show their knowledge in a short space of time. They

200

can also prove useful with shy students who are more reluctant to give extended responses in front of their peers.

For such students, who are desperate not to contribute lest they reveal their ignorance, we can deploy 'recognition questions'; that is to say, questions that include potential answers in the question, to lighten the degree of challenge. For example, in geography you may ask, 'Which part of the earth is directly below the crust: the mantle, the inner core or the outer core?'

We can probe their answer sensitively and, given their confidence is boosted, we can go on to probe their degree of understanding further. We may go on to build a sequence of questions, such as 'What were you thinking when you answered it was the mantle?' and 'Why do you think some students answer "outer core" by mistake?' Obviously, by probing the thinking of an individual student, we are encouraging others to think deeply about what they know and also 'how' and 'why' they came to know it too (more on this in the next chapter).

The 'recognition question' above clearly offered the student a multiple choice that can scaffold the thinking of our students. Dylan Wiliam, guru of feedback and formative assessment, offers the strategy of *hinge-point questions*.[6] This question type is multiple choice and therefore teachers can construct questions alongside answers that intentionally pose common misconceptions and errors. The hinge-point is the crucial element for Wiliam – because if the correct answer isn't known, he deems it unlikely that students will proceed successfully.

For example, when teaching the history of the Second World War, a teacher may ask the question:

What province was France looking to retain from Germany?

Confident questioning and feedback

A: The Sudetenland
B: Alsace and Lorraine
C: The Rhineland
D: Senegal

The answer is Alsace and Lorraine, but any errors may prove just as interesting in understanding the thinking of our students. The Sudetenland (the German name for areas in Czechoslovakia populated predominantly by German speakers) was indeed an area appropriated by the Nazis, so students would be familiar with the name. C and D also have relatedness to the World War and to France respectively. By selecting questions that could easily trip up students, it more precisely checks upon what students know.

We can go one step further and also question their degree of confidence in their answer with a 'confidence test', by explicitly offering them a further question to gauge their confidence level, such as:

How confident are you in your answer:

A: Highly confident
B: I am partially confident
C: I am guessing

If we wanted to mask the question somewhat, preventing students from giving us the answer they think we want to hear, we can make the 'confidence test' more implicit:

What province was France looking to retain from Germany?

A: The Sudetenland
B: Alsace and Lorraine
C: The Rhineland
D: A or B

E: A or C
F: B or C
G: Don't know

In probing their errors we may find out their faulty reasoning and be able to address it. This may prove more important than students getting the answer 'right'. We know that students overestimate how much they know. This is exacerbated when they are familiar with the material – the students will likely have learnt about the Rhineland when studying the Second World War. It gives them a sense of partial access to the answer that fuels them with overconfidence.

This simple strategy of hinge questions, alongside a 'confidence test', is really helpful as you can diagnose student understanding and identify misconceptions, whilst also noting where they are overconfident and wrong. We know that everybody finds it hard to dispense with misconceptions that compromise their beliefs. These simple 'confidence tests' get to the root of overconfidence so that we can better tackle it.

A 'confidence test' can be used for a standard classroom examination or an essay, giving us more useful information, on not only their answer, but how well executed they think their answer is too. More generally, getting students to monitor their confidence levels, and sharing them with their teacher, gives us powerful information to better modify our practice.

Good questioning, it would appear, can prove the ideal weapon against overconfidence, for both students and the teacher. As teachers, we can be that little bit more confident in what they know and understand, as well as how confidently they *think* they understand it.

Useful teaching strategies for highly effective questioning:

- **Key questions as learning objectives.** What better way to foster a culture of inquiry than to spark the whole shooting match off with a big question that gets students thinking critically about what they are going to learn?
- **Pose – pause – pounce – bounce.** This is a brilliantly simple and useful strategy. First, *pose* the question. Then *pause* (remembering the importance of 'wait time' in enhancing the quality of student answers), before you *pounce* with your question. The final *bounce* – bouncing the question, and answers, around different students in the class – is also crucial in that students are expected to constructively build upon the ideas of one another.
- **Graphic organisers.** You can help students consider the thinking process behind their answer by using graphic organisers to explore their answer to your question. For example, if a question offers two related but distinct answers, you could choose to use a Venn diagram to explore the answer. It provides a concrete visual aid that can better visualise the logic of the answer. You could extend this further by getting students to graphically organise their answers in a style of their choosing. A quick Google search for graphic organisers will reveal a plethora of options.
- **Give us a clue.** Sometimes a question can have a whole class stumped. You can ease the fear of being directly asked such a tricky question by offering the opportunity of a clue to the answer. Often, students may think they have the right answer, but they are hesitant for fear of making a mistake in front of their peers. Given a small clue or prompt, students can feel more confident in taking a guess or offering up a tentative response.
- **If this is the answer...what is the question?** Taken from the *Mock the Week* television show, this simple little technique sparks the inquisitiveness within

students – just by quickly flipping the standard question-and-answer format to deepen their thinking. Give them the answer and let them work backwards to defining a good question. It could be a relatively closed answer, like '3.14159265359' (the numerical value of pi); or something more open and abstract, like 'religion' (a potential powder keg).

Strategies for getting students to ask better questions

If you go looking for a quote for anything then Einstein is usually a safe bet. Einstein also attracts some great stories. One such story claims that his mother always asked him, 'What questions did you ask today?' rather than the usual, 'What did you do in school today?' We know where that got him: Nobel Prize winning global genius status. Everyone starts somewhere on the path to Nobel prize winning by asking good questions, we just don't all reach the heights of Einstein.

As a father of two beautiful children, I quickly learnt to better appreciate that children are powerhouses of curiosity: 'Daddy, why is the sky blue? Daddy, why are poppies red?' Learning about the world by asking *why* questions are just about one of the most natural states for all children. Here, my son is sitting in the back seat of the car making sense of the chaotic world flying by the window. My son doesn't yet comprehend why he should ask *why* questions (a later metacognitive state so crucial to learning), he just instinctively attempts to make sense with *why*.

Asking such deeper questions are important because, put simply, they make you more intelligent. By asking *why* questions – rather grandly described as 'elaborate interrogation' by cognitive scientists – students can actually make new knowledge stick and make it more

205

memorable. By asking questions about their new knowledge they become more *active learners*, which, again, aids how well they can recall what they have learned. The questions elaborate upon what they are learning, hooking the knowledge more deeply in their long-term memory, ploughing a deeper mental furrow in the child's mind.

Despite being naturally inclined to ask such questions, students ask relatively few in the classroom setting. In fact, it takes six to seven hours for a typical student to ask a single question in class.[7]

Perhaps it is less surprising when we consider in a class full of anything from twenty to thirty inquisitive students that there is relatively little direct questioning of the teacher in class. Some students hog the attention of the teacher, skewing the balance of such questioning still further.

Compare this to over twenty-six questions from the same archetypal student in a *one-to-one tutoring* session. The numbers are striking. With this data it makes it even more essential to ensure that all students ask effective questions.

Useful teaching strategies for getting students to ask great questions:

- **Just one more question...** Given any topic or subject, students can work collaboratively in groups to create an array of quality questions. They can then be given a series of challenging question stems to broaden their range of questions, such as the following: *What if... Suppose we knew... What would change if...?* As the topic develops, students can add 'just one more question', as well as answering the initial questions as their understanding grows.

- **Socratic questioning and Socratic circles.** The old dog really can teach us new tricks. Socrates himself believed that questioning was at the root of all learning and it is hard to disagree. The six steps of Socratic questioning facilitate a critical atmosphere that probes thinking and once more gets the students questioning in a structured way. There are six main categories:

  Q1 Get your students to clarify their thinking, such as: 'Can you explain it further?'

  Q2 Challenging students about their assumptions, such as: 'Is your answer taking account of X?'

  Q3 Evidence as a basis for their argument, such as: 'Can you give me examples that support your argument?'

  Q4 Explore counter arguments and different perspectives, such as: 'Who would challenge this argument and why?'

  Q5 Explore implications and consequences, such as: 'What would happen if Z?'

  Q6 Question the question, such as: 'Why did we start with this question?'

- **Question continuum.** The continuum involves the students first devising questions, either individually, in pairs or groups, on any given topic or idea. Then the continuum is created very visibly, either on the whiteboard, or more semi-permanently on a display board (which is a great way to repeat the strategy in future lessons). The horizontal axis would represent the *Interest Level* generated by each question and the vertical axis could represent *Complexity* (from closed, factual questions to open, conceptual questions). Students could feed back their opinions, shaped by the teacher, to identify the best questions – which then could be the subject of further exploration.

- **Questioning monitor.** This strategy constructively involves students in the evaluation and reflection of the questioning process. A monitor, or a pair of monitors, would be given the responsibility to track and monitor the frequency of questions: teacher and student – open or closed; factual or conceptual. You can have them monitor for a given task, or relate more cumulative research by undertaking the monitoring over a week or two of lessons.

- **The question wall.** This is a working space for students to communicate questions about their learning. Giving students Post-it® notes and asking them to commit questions in writing typically eliminates those questions that reflect a sense of 'learned helplessness'. To add a level of nuance to the wall, consider creating simple quadrants with simple labels. Students can be advised that closed questions are placed on the left of the wall, with more open questions to the right. A vertical axis could indicate the time the student would expect was needed to support them: placing questions that need a high degree of support, and time, higher up the wall.

The power of feedback

A confident learner needs to know where they are going, what the standard of success looks like, and what they need to do to meet that high standard. The teacher needs to facilitate this state of affairs. Feedback is an essential tool to help make this happen.

The problem is that most discussions of feedback in schools move quickly to written assessments and examinations. Let's be clear: feedback is so much more than simply written marking of an examination or similar.

By obsessing about summative tests, we can too easily miss the most important assessment going on inside the classroom: what is going on inside the head of the student. Understanding what is going on inside their head is crucial and we can tease it out through questions and dialogue, both verbally and in written form.

We begin to ask ourselves some important questions: does the student know what excellence looks like? Do they know how to make changes and improvements to reach that standard? Can they seek out feedback on how to make those improvements and get better?

All the available evidence points to the fact that feedback works. It is top of the tree; the king of teaching strategies. We just need more of it, right? The problem is that feedback is a complex thing and teachers are too often unclear about what we specifically mean when we use the term feedback, the best way to go about it, or exactly how much feedback to give to have the desired impact.

The most effective summary of feedback distils it into three clear questions that should go on inside the head of our students:

Where am I going?
How am I going?
Where to next?[8]

If a student can answer these three questions competently then they can be more confident that they are on the right track. Feedback is clearly much more than just 'solely about correctness.'[9] It is about closing the gap between what is understood and what we want them to understand. This isn't just about feedback on the students' task either – it could be apt feedback on their effort and motivation, or on how well they are thinking about a problem or their working together in collaboration.

We too easily misjudge feedback as an end point, or a summative judgement, thereby staring in the rear-view mirror of assessment. In reality, good feedback is all around us in each and every lesson. It is dynamic:

encapsulating the past, present and the future of our students' learning.

Schools, driven by those who judge them, can often concentrate upon written feedback because it is visible and more easily measurable. Sadly, too often, this is about enforcing compliance from teachers rather than improving the learning of our students.

There is an obvious problem. Aiming to improve the quality of learning after it has happened too often lacks the requisite emotional immediacy for our students and it can lack the impact our time and effort deserves. We need to assure the quality of learning as it happens, most often with immediate oral feedback in class, rather than retrospectively with written feedback.

Clues in the etymology of the word 'assessment' can better guide us here. From the Latin verb *assidere*, meaning 'to sit beside', we are shown that rather than simply considering feedback as something we write about in summative fashion, feedback should be predominantly formative. By 'sitting beside' our students we are making active and instantaneous judgements that feed forward to 'Where to next?'.

We know that as soon as students see their work labelled with a mark or a grade, they can ignore their diagnostic feedback. Simply slapping a grade onto their work does not help students to know what to do better next time.

Instead, we need to prompt forward-facing action. We can give *reminder prompts* ('How can you improve the accuracy of this passage?'); *scaffold prompts* ('include a wider range of punctuation here – including a question mark'), and *example prompts* ('choose one of these sentence starters to add depth to your response...') to aid the process and to help students respond in manageable steps. We need to prompt action and hard thinking.

In clear language, we can give our students guidance and goals to move forward. If we can break those goals down into manageable actions, then we can better foster motivation. We need to set clear, actionable *proximal goals* (those goals that are discrete and short-term in nature) linked to *distal goals* (big-picture goals that are achieved in the long-term).

Consider it like the piecing together of a jigsaw. Students can give up when faced with one hundred pieces piled high, but give them feedback on each singular step; linking piece to piece (the proximal goal), they can gradually see the ultimate endgame of the completed jigsaw (the distal goal).

Take a moment to apply this model to a topic with a class: What is the big picture? What big questions underlie the learning? How can you best break that down into the knowledge and skills required into smaller, accessible actions.

It isn't all plain sailing. Students often misunderstand our feedback. We need to be vigilant and check their understanding of the goals we set and, most crucially, give them the time and resources to act upon them. Too often, we can focus on what the teacher does (the input) and forget the positive impact from feedback actually derives from what the students think and do (the student output).

I've been overconfident about my feedback. I have set questionnaires that have revealed that the written feedback, the subject of my painstaking labour, simply wasn't understood. My students simply didn't want to embarrass themselves, or me, by saying so.

We should all be asking ourselves whether our approach to feedback is as effective as it could be.

We should also be mindful that students will give feedback to one another at each stage of the process, regardless of what we do or say, even when we think that we are in control. Graham Nuthall captured this in his research,[10] showing that students get about 80 per cent of their feedback from their peers. You won't be surprised to hear – they give such feedback with great confidence, but they are usually wrong!

This doesn't mean that peer feedback is a failure. In fact, it indicates something quite the opposite: we really need to better manage the mass of peer feedback in our classroom.

Peer feedback can too often be derided as being a poor excuse for teacher feedback. Of course, if students are given minimal training then they will do peer feedback badly, but if we invest time in training them up, then the learning gains could be immense.

The teacher can never give every individual student the requisite feedback all the time, so we need to employ the power of peers, with clear parameters of what good feedback looks like and sounds like. We can then at least be more confident that the unsolicited feedback they dole out is at least of a decent quality.

Useful strategies to enhance the quality of feedback in the classroom:

- **ABC feedback.** Oral feedback and discussion between students makes up much of the core business of the classroom. Done well, it is disciplined and graceful and makes for great feedback. We can do it better by giving a little more structure. The strategy is simple: A stands for 'Agree with...', B for 'Build upon...' and C for 'Challenge...'. It really is easy; for example: 'James, Helen has stated her view of Hamlet's character – do you want to A, B or C?' Once this structure is part of the fabric of group talk, then students can readily give clear feedback to their peers. Challenging ideas and giving constructive criticism quickly becomes part of the healthy norm.
- **Stripped back feedback.** This idea is a time-saver for teachers giving written feedback, but it works because it

gets students working harder and thinking more actively about their feedback. Simply strip away all the language from your written feedback on their work. You may choose to colour code your feedback, or use a few symbols instead – with an appropriate key to define their meaning, but ultimately you want students to struggle a little and have to think harder. If a passage of their writing, or an item in their design project is colour-coded red, then students are forced to work out how to improve. Make them work harder so that you don't have to!

- **Wedding-cake feedback.** This is a simple analogy to make the layers of assessment clear. The first layer of the wedding cake is self-assessment. They need to be trained to understand what they're looking for and understand the huge value of self-assessment. It is the biggest tier for a reason: they should spend the most time assessing what they have done first. The second tier, taking slightly less time, is peer assessment. Finally, the smallest tier, atop the cake, is teacher assessment. We simply go about assessing their assessment and that of their peers with some expert quality control.

- **Now try... Explain why...** After giving written feedback we need to make sure that we have students actively responding to that feedback. A nice and simple habit is to use the phrase 'Now try... Explain why...' in your verbal or written feedback.

- **Feedback codes.** How many times have you found yourself writing the same feedback to half of your class? Instead of being mired in a mass of written feedback, create a simple symbol code for the most common errors and misconceptions. Label their work using the key to the symbol code. If you have the flexibility, students can group together and act on their feedback in groups with the shared code.

A focus on failure

How we deal with failure matters and how our students respond to emotional setbacks matters just as much.

When we deal with the fragile emotions of our students we can tend toward praise and to instinctively protect our students from the harsh exposure of being faced with failure. It is only natural. This delicate management of emotion can, however, compromise the process of giving accurate feedback. The problem is that this approach can have the opposite effect to what is desired. Shielded from failure and lavished with praise, students develop a sense that they should avoid failure and risk at all cost, and their entire fledgling identity can depend upon it.

A fear of failure can have a corrosive effect on the learning of our students. We all know students who will go a long way to mask their fear of failure, from telling their peers that they didn't revise for a test, or setting their goals too low to avoid looking stupid. At the root of it, it is about masking their fears of looking unintelligent in front of their peers. It is an unconfident act of self-preservation.

Carol Dweck, with her decades of research on students, their mindsets and attitudes to failure, has shown that if we praise students with person-orientated feedback, such as 'you're a really talented musician, well done', then we can subtly invoke the brittle ego of the student. They quickly begin to invest their identity in success and they will studiously avoid failure in their mistaken belief that their success is down to their 'natural' gifts.

Dweck argues, in stark contrast, that students given process praise, such as 'a strong effort with that song – you're really working on your range', can better help students understand that success is dependent upon their efforts during the process of learning. We have all heard it in our classrooms: 'I'm no good at [insert subject of choice]'.

This attitude shuts down any necessity to pay proper attention to the feedback.

Feedback becomes useful when such personal fears are dissipated, or at least better managed. We become receptive to taking a risk and making changes that may well not pan out. It is those experiences when we push our boundaries that we learn the most: students need to feel this experience to grow their confidence.

Encouraging the right attitude from our students is important, but it is no easy feat and will likely take time.

We need to be careful we focus on the right type of confidence here. If students see their success as fixed and dependent on their 'natural' intelligence, then their confidence will be built on loose foundations. In the face of failure they will crumble. The confidence we need to cultivate in our students is that anybody can learn and improve if they invest effort and focus on the right strategies to get better.

Here are some useful strategies to strip away the stigma of failure in the classroom:

- **My favourite mistake.** Back in 1998, Sheryl Crow sang about her 'favourite mistake'. Which of her famous ex-boyfriends is the subject of the tune is unclear, but you can harness inspiration from this pop gem to normalise failure for any set of student answers to a given topic. There are a variety of tools for doing this. Circulating the room and selecting your favourite mistake is a lo-fi option. Getting students to write their own mistakes on cue cards or whiteboards works just as well. For the technologically minded, displaying a mistake on a visualizer for the whole class to see – and then exploring the misconception – does the trick brilliantly. You can unpick these failures and learn from them.
- **Finding failure.** Students are most often focused in their pursuit of the right answer, but offer them the

opportunity to find mistakes and errors, and they are relentless. You can use an error-strewn passage, or a faulty product, to help students seek out errors. Rather than having ten answers, with ticks or crosses, tell the student that five of these answers are wrong and get them honing in on the failure. Subtly, failure quickly becomes accepted as a natural part of learning.

- **Prototyping.** In subject areas like design technology, the notion of prototyping is a given. A prototype, of course, is a preliminary version of a product. It is helpful to explain the notion of prototyping and how inventors learn from their failures (many useful stories attend this topic, such as how the light-bulb invention didn't prove anything like a light-bulb moment). Across the curriculum, students are busy prototyping, crafting and drafting essays, sketching drafts in art etc. We need to make this process visible and explicit. Get students taking photos of their prototypes, create classroom displays of their prototypes, and get them explaining their design process – failures and all.

- **Famous failures.** Every subject discipline is littered with notable failures that led to successes. From artists ahead of their time, to world-changing scientific discoveries like penicillin, inadvertently invented in a dirty laboratory. We need to bring these intriguing stories to light – rightly associating failure as a requirement on the path to success.

- **Bog standard to brilliant.** One of the issues with peer feedback is that students often worry about what their friends will think, or about their own competence in giving feedback. Model constructive feedback, whilst making light of peer feedback, by offering a pretty dour effort of your own (fabricated of course – you are no doubt brilliant). Given your model, get students to feedback on the work, you can then scaffold their feedback, highlighting when they do it well and clarifying when they don't. Do beware: students love nothing more than to give their teachers a dose of healthy criticism.

IN SHORT...

- Questioning is the oxygen of effective teaching. We must give it more of our attention: planning, crafting and trialling questions and question sequences.
- We must allow students time to think hard when we ask a question...wait for it.... hold on...a little more...yes – now – about five seconds should do it.
- We need to train our students to ask good questions. When they ask us hard, challenging questions, we can be more confident that they have the right tools to go on learning.
- Good feedback works very effectively. Bad feedback is, well, ineffective. No surprises so far! What is crucial is that we know the difference and we understand what makes good feedback. In a sentence, *good feedback gets students to think hard and act to improve.*
- We need to help our students recognise that failure is normal – in fact, a prerequisite of effective learning and success. If we create the right classroom culture then we can still breed confidence and competence, even in the face of failure, or even because of it.

Notes

1 Leven, T. and Long, R. (1981), 'Effective instruction', Washington, DC: Association for Supervision and Curriculum Development.
2 Ausubel, D. (1968), *Educational Psychology: A Cognitive View*, p. vi. New York: Holt, Rinehart and Winston.
3 Hattie, J. (2012), *Visible Learning for Teachers: Maximising Impact on Learning*, p. 30. London: Routledge.
4 Rowe, M. (1986), 'Wait time: slowing down may be a way of speeding up!' *Journal of Teacher Education*, 1: 37–43.
5 Stiles, W.B., Putnam, S.M., Wolf, M.H. and James, S.A. (1979), 'Verbal response mode profiles of patients and physicians in medical screening interviews', *International Journal of Medical Education*, 54: 81–89.
6 Wiliam, D. (2011), *Embedded Formative Assessment*, Bloomington: Solution Tree Press.
7 Graesser, A.C. and Person, N.K. (1994), 'Question asking during tutoring'. *American Educational Research Journal*, 31(1): 104–137.
8 Hattie, J. and Timperley, H. (2007), 'The power of feedback', *Review of Educational Research*, 77 (1): 81–112.
9 Hattie, J. and Timperley, H. (2007), 'The power of feedback', *Review of Educational Research*, 77 (1): 81–112.
10 Nuthall, G. (2007), *The Hidden Lives of Learners*, Wellington: NZCER Press.

13 Successful modelling and metacognition

James is sitting at the front of my English class. He is eager to please and the prospect of narrative writing – of the gothic variety – fills him with earnest glee. The task is set: write the opening of a gothic novel.

Each student is guided to meticulously plan their writing: marshalling their ideas and some gothic delights into good order. Mind maps are drawn and checklists are devised.

For James, the race begins. In a flurry, unburdened by planning, mind maps or checklists, he races headlong into the excitement of his blood-stained gothic imagination. He begins writing and he simply doesn't stop. His piling up of errors doesn't deter him nor slow him down. No calls for careful crafting and drafting inhibit his impassioned efforts.

James finishes in record time. Many students are still shaping their openings sentences as James proudly announces he is 'done'. Despite having ample time to check through his writing, he cannot muster the inspiration to check or draft it. He protests that it is definitely finished. His glee soon fizzles and he goes seeking out praise.

The problem here has been played out in too many of my lessons to mention. James will not be happy with his feedback. He has bypassed the three crucial steps of *planning, monitoring* and *evaluating* his work, so his feedback will inevitably fall short of his expectations.

So how do we maintain the demonstrable enthusiasm shown by James, whilst getting him to think harder and to work more effectively? How do we help the likes of James to navigate and persist through the challenges of crafting and drafting, confronting and conquering failure and mistakes at each step?

The answer is training James to think with an academic mindset that would better guide his learning, bolstering him with the skills that foster resilience and confidence in the face of hurdles and setbacks. This will prove no quick fix. He may learn to plan well in English, but then he will struggle to transfer that skill over to his learning in geography. His geography teacher will need to train James in planning like a geographer. This takes time, effort and skill on behalf of the teacher, with significant commitment from James, but the perseverance will prove worth it.

Over forty years ago, John Flavell, an educational psychologist, popularised the term *metacognition* in educational circles. Put simply, it means *thinking about your own thinking*, and what Guy Claxton described as, 'knowing what to do when you don't know what to do'.[1] It is not a new idea – it is as old as teaching itself: think hard about your learning and act accordingly. It is the crucial and ongoing process of questioning, feedback and self-assessment going on inside the student's head.

Why then is metacognition not front and centre of our focus on effective teaching and learning?

Metacognition, admittedly, sounds fuzzy – like some fly-by-night educational fad blowing through an interminably long teacher-training day. Sometimes teacher training is rammed so full of jargon that we can easily become immune to it. We can all nod along sagely in agreement: 'Yes – getting students to think about their thinking – of course. I do that all the time.' It is particularly ripe for being dismissed as stating the bleedin' obvious, but we need to persist beyond our instinctive cynicism, getting beneath the terminology and breaking it down into a process of useful, manageable actions in the classroom.

Subject domains most often provide us with the frameworks of knowledge that help build understanding and meaning; yet, crucially, our students also need to understand *what to do* with their subject knowledge and *how* to mould and adapt it to fit what is required.

Metacognition is essential because it can provide students with strategies to deploy their subject knowledge with confidence. They can think like artists, scientists and more. For James, it can help him better think like a writer, and it will make all the difference to his gothic story.

Metacognition: Steps to success

Metacognition then is as easy as one, two, three: *planning, monitoring* and *evaluation*.

1. Planning

First, this thinking about thinking starts with high-quality planning. Our novice students too often neglect this important stage. We need to slow them down, breaking the task down, so that they can reach a deeper level of understanding of what they need to do.

It can be devilishly hard to get a young student like James to plan a piece of extended writing, but persevere we must. We need to explicitly model learning and thinking such as using visualisation tools like graphic organisers, concept maps, flow charts, Venn diagrams and more.

The planning phase sees students like James marshal their resources. They can ask the questions deployed intuitively by experts: what prior knowledge do I need to undertake this task? What type of planning process will help best: a checklist or a mind map? What examples can I draw upon to guide me toward success? How much time do I have? Where should I start?

Effectively, metacognition is a process of self-explanation. Our feedback and explanations are no doubt important, but how our students interpret it and enact it will prove key. For James, it is a process of question and answer, simultaneously drawing from his knowledge and the support of the teacher. We can help the process along by prompting the questions that James and his peers will need to answer to be successful.

2. Monitoring

The hard thinking doesn't stop amidst the act of writing either. James must then slow down and monitor his efforts. He may consult his well-crafted plan, or check the parameters of the task: what techniques does he need to include? What proofreading checks does he need to undertake?

During this phase students like James will keep posing themselves questions to tweak and improve what they do. They can ask: am I on the right track? Have I made any mistakes? What was I asked to focus on in my previous round of feedback? Do I have any typical failings I need to be vigilant for? What do I do if I am stuck? What do I need to do next?

Of course, the better our students have planned, the easier it is for them to monitor how they are doing. If they use support tools, like using a checklist, it frees students like James up to think about the trickier questions that attend his learning.

All three of the steps of metacognition are inextricably linked and a student may revisit the different steps in a complex dance. It is down to us to supply the expert choreography.

3. Evaluation

Finally, the finish line approaches and victory is within reach. Most students have exhausted their will and motivation – they're 'done' they tell us. Then we have the tricky task of mustering yet more of the will and skill of our students to then check and thoroughly evaluate their work. We are effectively slowing students down and encouraging them to reflect upon their learning, but this isn't natural or easy.

After the rush of action, our brains, and those of our students, instinctively lose some interest and motivation. We need to help our students better reflect and conquer their desire for a quick and easy finish. They need to reflect, draft, tweak and refine.

They need to ask: how well did I do? Did I match the success criteria and complete my checklist? Is there anything I have missed? Do I need to go back and fix any errors or make any additions? Is this the best possible version I can do?

Successful modelling and metacognition

Let's place James in the different scenario of an art lesson, undertaking a still-life painting. He needs to revisit the same thinking loop of planning, monitoring and evaluating, but he needs to deploy the thinking of an artist (and I don't mean lopping his ear off in frustration). He would ask once more:

What resources do I need?
What prior knowledge can I draw upon?
Am I clear what I have to do?
How many planning sketches are enough?
Am I going to create an accurate representation, or use an abstract style?
What strategies can I employ to enhance my use of colour?
How do I best correct an error in my sketch?
Is my palate right for the job?
Does my painting match my plan and is there anything I may have missed?
Is my painting an improvement on my previous efforts?

As you can see, the knowledge and skills required are different for each respective subject discipline, but the to-and-fro of self-questioning and hard thinking are similar across the span of the curriculum.

Try it yourself: consider a task, like planning a lesson or initiating a lesson first thing in the morning, before then going about watching yourself think. It feels a bit odd, but give it a go.

What are your steps? What planning and monitoring do you undertake? Do you have time to evaluate? By becoming more conscious about our thinking processes we refine our actions, we defy overconfidence and we move a small step toward the status of the confident expert.

Getting students thinking independently

All this talk of getting students to ask themselves questions and monitor their learning reminds me of the much talked about notion of *independent learning*. The idea of a class full of hard-thinking, self-motivated students, all taking full responsibility for their learning, is surely a tempting nirvana for teachers everywhere.

If metacognition is getting students to consciously think about their thinking, then independent learning is the logical end point. Students, having internalised the metacognitive processes, are then able to use them independently and with confidence.

And yet, the vaunted promise of successful independent learning rarely materialises.

Perhaps it is because we are doing it wrong, or we are misunderstanding the notion of independent learning?

No doubt, there is a common confusion about exactly what we mean when we define independent learning. It is too often caricatured and associated with *discovery learning* or the vague notion of *personalisation*. In the mode of 'discovery learning' – often depicted as students working on their own, finding their own problems and devising their own solutions – the role of the teacher is sidelined as inessential, a mere spare part.

Too quickly we dispense with the expertise of the teacher and we too easily demean the value of 'teacher talk'. We forget a simple truth: without a great deal of prior knowledge, and the expert support of the teacher, successful independent learning doesn't happen effectively. It is the talk and dialogue, instigated, structured and led by the teacher, that best facilitates independent learning.

Without being supported through their thinking and their work, our students are too easily overwhelmed[2] and they lose all confidence.

Successful modelling and metacognition

Before James can ask himself questions and lead his own learning, he needs supportive prompts and such questions modelled for him over and over until they become something like a habit for him.

Of course, developing learning with the end goal of independence in mind requires that the teacher really knows their students. I need to know what makes James tick and how to coax him into making improvements and to better spot his mistakes. I can provide tailored help and scaffolding, before then subtly decreasing that support over time, and then expecting some independent thinking from James.

There is a delicate balance to be struck here. In the vast majority of cases as a teacher we don't expect independence – we expect *interdependence*. We explain, we direct, we question, we model, and we check the understanding of our students, before then guiding their practice. Finally, after a great deal of dependence, we encourage an increasing independence of thought, and yet more practice.

We can help students confidently lead their own learning, but the apprenticeship of students like James will fill most of his time in education. Metacognition will help provide the means, and independent learning will prove the desired end.

Take the commonplace example of taking a test. Students need to undertake proven revision strategies, such as using flashcards, taking quizzes and writing exam answers. They also need to get themselves organised, finding the right resources, before then simply sticking at it for a sustained period. All this takes time, willpower, and a series of metacognitive strategies. It also requires guidance and scaffolding. We need to model effective revision and motivate students to do it well.

At each step, we must model the metacognition required for success. When the test is complete, what then?

The natural thought process of the student could be 'the test is complete – I'm done'. We can combat this thinking by getting students to better evaluate their test performance.

Rather than their obsessing over a grade, we can ask questions like 'How well did you prepare for this test?' or 'How does your preparation and revision time equate with your exam performance?' to provoke thinking about how they performed and how they might improve in future. We can get our students better evaluating their performance in examinations, question by question, alongside their revision skill and application.

With better evaluation we can puncture the *illusion of knowing* – that is to say, their natural overconfidence having sat an examination, or undertaken any task. When students begin to internalise the process, then they can get nearer the desired destination: successful independent learning.

Useful strategies for successful (metacognitive) independent learning:

● **Exam wrappers.** A useful strategy that can enhance the staple diet of exam feedback is to 'wrap' the feedback with questions that more fully tease out a self-evaluation. For example, a sequence of questions you can ask students to complete when they have undertaken an assessment includes: what grade do you think you have achieved? How many hours revision did you commit to revising? What revision strategies did you deploy [supply them with a list] and how long did you spend on each strategy? By asking these evaluative questions it gets students monitoring and evaluating their own exam performance, but it also gives the teacher really useful information about how well students are learning. Do a quick Internet search for 'exam wrappers' and you will find some useful models. This Carnegie Mellon web page is a good start: www.cmu.edu/teaching/ designteach/teach/examwrappers/.

- **Pre-flight checklist.** Get students to check their planning and devise a thorough checklist that they can consult at each step of their learning. This provides a handy tool for their self-monitoring.
- **Triplicate note making.** Good note making is an important skill not to be left to chance. Too many students go through school without any direct instruction about how to do it most effectively. Unsurprisingly, self-questioning and hard thinking are involved. By getting students to ask questions about the information as they are making notes, as well as devising memorisation strategies, they can deepen their degree of understanding. Rather than your standard notes, get students to instead create three columns:

  Column 1: Core information. The key facts, information or quotes relevant to the topic at hand.

  Column 2: Key questions sparked by the information. Such conceptual 'how' and 'why' questions can help deepen their understanding.

  Column 3: Memorable images and mnemonics to help students consciously embed the core information into their memory.

- **Succinct summaries.** The skill of summarising is useful in all sorts of ways. Summarising an explanation; an argument; the chapter in a textbook; a sequence of skills – all requires practice and teacher guidance and modelling. Given any task of summarising, such as reading a chapter on a new topic for homework, get students to concisely summarise the material within a limited word count.
- **'How to' guides.** Students need structured support to thrive independently. If we expect that our students would complete a substantial activity or project

effectively, then we would need to make our success criteria explicit, giving appropriate tips and support. A 'How to' guide, either created by the teacher, or by the students in collaboration, can provide a valuable scaffold that can help them flourish when moving toward independence.

Self-regulation and thinking hard

What if we were immune to boredom and procrastination? Imagine what we could do. The nagging complaints of some of our more reluctant students would fade away.

Perhaps, given that 'boring' task, they would spend five more minutes working at it. Then ten minutes...then twenty. Before long, they may realise that it isn't boring at all.

A fundamental aspect of metacognition is the capacity to think about, and act upon, our capacity for self-control. Just as productivity matters for teachers, it is undoubtedly important for students too. We need to help our students recognise how to stick at a task and how to fend off boredom and procrastination.

Telling our students to get on with it, or 'just work harder' patently won't work. We need to furnish them with the strategies to better structure their thinking processes and to better plan their learning and more.

Self-regulation and self-control, particularly during the emotional storm of puberty and the teenage years, is something like a Holy Grail for teachers and parents alike.

We know that the teen brain is prone to risk-taking, acute self-consciousness and weak self-control. Right at the point that teachers are looking to help strengthen the self-regulation of our students, helping them to think harder, for longer, the biological changes happening in the brains of our students are battling against us.

Adolescence is a crucial age for development of the pre-frontal cortex (right at the front of the brain, just behind the forehead), which is so critical in the brain for our decision-making, planning and the management of our emotions. We know that this awkward and problematic development means that teenagers can make lots of poor judgements, with seemingly simple tasks like planning their homework proving devilishly difficult.

The fight parents face with their child over homework, or when our students clash with their teachers, can prove stark evidence of the rapidly changing teen brain and how it can inhibit our students' thinking when it comes to getting organised to learn well.

How children relate to others during adolescence becomes especially important as such brain changes mean that children begin to care more about the perceptions of their peers than their parents or teachers.[3] When students see failure and exerting effort as a threat to how their peers view them, this can prove corrosive for learning. In short, they stop thinking productively.

We return to two of Bandura's sources of self-efficacy: observing one another and social persuasion. Our students are sensitively prone to observing, mimicking and following the herd when it comes to their peers, in the classroom and beyond. We need to ensure that we are deftly guiding the herd, almost imperceptibly, by supporting, shaping and cajoling the path of their thinking and action. We need to persuade entire groups of students that sticking to the task and thinking hard will lead to success.

We need to make tasks like planning 'normal' or make doing your homework the done thing amongst the group. With small behaviour nudges we can do the trick. By spotlighting students doing activities, such as planning homework well on a regular basis, we begin to normalise them for students, helping them to be more confident in acting academically.

We can help by shattering some unhelpful myths about how we think best, with students, parents and teachers alike.

Take our alleged ability, or that of our students, to multitask, or the belief that the brain has been irrevocably changed by modern technology. These are predominantly myths. We should recognise this, sharing this knowledge, before giving them some much-needed training on how to better focus when they are learning. Being logged into social media, listening to their favourite music and with the television flickering in the background, our students won't learn effectively. Crucially, we need to show them how they can.

Beating boredom, focusing and simply being able to better concentrate, remain fundamental prerequisites for hard thinking, and therefore, school success.

Useful strategies for self-regulation and fending off boredom:

- **If...then...strategies.** Often we are most vulnerable to distraction and boredom before we get started on a task. To get the ball rolling, and to resist learned helplessness from students, provide them with a prompt list for likely hurdles when undertaking a complex task. This could be in the form of 'If...then... strategies' – that is to say, handy reminders about how they can overcome common hurdles and get unstuck with some independence.
- **Visual timers.** We can more consciously use visual timers regularly so that students can learn to self-regulate their learning with a good sense of timing (remember, we are all bad at judging how long it will take to complete a task successfully), whilst drawing upon the energy and good stress (remember eustress?) of a time deadline.

- **Spotlighting.** Keep up the pace of the lesson and provide meaningful breaks in the learning to shine a 'spotlight' on a singular student, or group, and display their learning. In art, for example, it could be gathering the whole class to observe a particularly strong painting, before talking about it and breaking down the steps that led to such excellence – an apt example of metacognition in action. It also gives students a welcome mental break from the intensity of the hard thinking necessary when undertaking their own work.

- **Paint the big picture.** Keep restating the big picture of the learning – the long-term goal. This reminds students of their motivation for concentration and hard thinking. Enlighten students why their lazy brains see them 'give in to feel good' with a quick fix – like delving into their social media timeline – and share with them the science of why they are prone to distraction and boredom.

- **Peer effort awards.** Focus on the intrinsic reward of a job well done, but also shine a light on outstanding displays of effort and focused hard work. You can secretly nominate a different student each week to monitor the effort levels of their peers. This can result in student-led awards (ideally, of the intrinsic kind – James worked the hardest, so his great work will be his reward). Quite quickly, students recognise that effort is privileged over seeming natural ability, and they can be better motivated to fight off a barrage of boredom or distraction.

Modelling expertise

From our earliest experiences, we learn, think and behave by example. Many of us can draw upon rich memories from our childhood whereat one of our parents, or grandparents, taught us how to bake a cake, paint the fence, or build the perfect sandcastle (sadly, some students cannot and we should be mindful of this).

Our role models matter. The patient guidance of being taught by an expert can prove an indelible memory. Many of us have a teacher who still shines in our memory for this reason.

Albert Bandura, our guru of self-efficacy, is also famed for a memorable psychological experiment, undertaken back in 1961, on the subject of role-model behaviour – nicknamed the 'Bobo doll experiment'.[4] The experiment included seventy-two children who were exposed to adult role models, either being aggressive, or not, with a Bobo doll (an inflatable doll, about five feet high, which bounces back when knocked over) and a mallet, before then being given time to play with the doll.

The results: children exposed to aggressive adult models showed more aggression in their 'play'.

This experiment, and the results, have been debated for half a century, but the notion that how we think and behave in social situations is affected by those around us is a given. We live and learn through example – good or ill. Rather than the violence inspired by the 'Bobo doll experiment', teachers should seek out the modelling of academic (and social) excellence at every juncture possible. Our behaviour management should be founded on this premise: the behaviours we exhibit should be those that we want our students to enact.

My all-time favourite teaching strategy, as an English teacher, is 'shared writing'. This strategy is the process of undertaking writing with the students. In effect, it is 'metacognition live'. I collaboratively plan the writing with the class, making audible the thinking process of a writing expert (well, at least in relation to my students). I then make a start, again talking through my thinking processes, making instantaneous decisions and revisions.

233

Successful modelling and metacognition

The process of 'shared writing' is so effective because it models the assured thinking and metacognitive processes we want our students to imitate, but it can also exemplify the mistakes and failures that attend 'real' learning. When writing on the board, students speedily note an error. Unabashed, I make the change and offer the explanation that such errors and failures are wholly natural.

Ironically, some teachers lack confidence in undertaking shared writing in case it sees them make a mistake, when actually this occurrence, which shows that mistakes happen in all learning, may prove the most valuable aspect of the task for our students.

The deft to and fro of questioning during 'shared writing' can harness the collective knowledge of the group, whilst laying bare some misconceptions or gaps in their knowledge. By asking, 'What word should I use here?' we probe to see if they grasp the purpose of our writing, or by asking 'What is the problem here?' we ascertain their problem solving capacity in the thick of writing.

One of the favourite lessons I have observed outside of my subject area in recent years was an art lesson. The core of the lesson was the teacher sketching a self-portrait. The steady, step-by-step guide, aided by a clear explanation of the 'why' and the 'how', was quite simply a tour de force. After a few questions, students spent an age rapt in their own efforts, with full understanding of the excellence expected and how to best attain it.

When a student follows a teacher modelling the learning, they are trained to better understand what they know, identify the gaps in their knowledge, and deploy strategies in the pursuit of excellence.

When faced with disastrous mock examination results for his economics class, John Tomsett, my colleague and head teacher at Huntington School, knew that he had to model the basic processes that made for exam success: 'I knew they had learned the theory I had taught them, they just had no idea, under examination conditions, how to apply what they knew to an examination question. They could not think their way through the examination paper.'

John wanted his students to think more effectively under the pressure of exam conditions. He used a past exam paper, but not in the conventional way. Rather than model the actual answers himself, he walked them through just how to *think* through an exam, exploring his metacognitive processes: 'When I am tested my brain goes into a state of high alert and I wanted to model my thinking in real time to my students. They had a blank copy of the paper and I insisted that they wrote down what I wrote down, verbatim. "Don't waffle" was a mantra which appeared across each page of my annotated paper!'

John's economics students began to perform in examinations better than ever before. It proved a useful example of how we need to teach our students fundamentally how to think, especially when faced with potentially confidence-sapping scenarios like examinations.

Learning by example

Fostering an appetite for excellence for our students can change their thinking. By modelling excellence, whilst expecting no less from them, we create a culture of high expectations that can have a profound effect on learning.

We can of course guide students to the best that has been thought and said in our subject discipline. An art teacher would no doubt utilise the great artists in their teaching; yet, as we inspire students with the genius of Michelangelo or Picasso, we need to instruct using the accessible model of students just like them – errors and all.

Providing good examples may actually prove less useful than using contrasting examples that prove 'near misses' and 'not quite good enough'.[5] By challenging students to identify the flaws in these 'near misses', we get them thinking hard about the exact qualities that define 'excellence'.

We can too quickly resort to using rubrics (criteria for teachers and/or students to define success) that describe excellence, but this can prove abstract and difficult for many of our students to understand. For example, 'use of vocabulary that displays flair and originality' can prove pretty vague and useless to our students. Instead, showing them multiple examples of writing that exhibit interesting vocabulary choices is much more concrete and meaningful, whilst providing students with some ready-made ideas.

In the act of comparing such models, our students internalise an understanding of the ingredients of success. By crafting a range of models and examples, making concrete our expectations of 'excellence', we provide the stuff of real assessment – the crucial assessment that goes on inside the heads of our students.

We need to take care with our modelling. As models are so supportive of our thinking, students can become dependent upon the models we provide. Therefore, we need to deftly remove this scaffold over time, omitting models when required, or reintroducing them when they are needed.

James would no doubt benefit from reading passages of brilliant gothic prose, but he could too easily become prone to imitation, thereby stifling his creativity and potentially even stunting his unique excellence.

Useful modelling strategies to make excellence visible in the classroom:

- **Live feedback.** Many teachers spend a huge chunk of their time giving written feedback. All too often, students don't quite understand our pointers or they wilfully ignore it. We can help students think more academically by giving feedback to one student (a sensitive selection process is of course required), either using a visualizer, or by photographing their work, or simply talking it through with the group. This is a good task to precede students reviewing the examples of their peers.

- **Multiple modelling.** Students benefit from thinking hard about the nuanced differences between examples – sometimes the more subtle the differences, the better. By classifying and defining what exemplars are better, and why, it can really deepen their understanding and refine their thinking. They can work collaboratively, or in pairs, to sort and stratify a group of model answers or problems. They quickly become much more confident and competent in then self-assessing their own learning and making improvements.

- **Gallery critique.** This is a strategy borrowed from American educationalist Ron Berger. It describes the process of setting up the room like a 'gallery' that displays the work of our students. Their peers then give 'specific, kind and helpful' feedback on their draft work (this could be completed on Post-it® notes attached to the work). This task is doubly beneficial for our students. By exposing them to multiple models it gives them an opportunity to survey good ideas, but they also receive specific feedback on their own work.

- **Think alouds.** Students can often classify and critique a given example, but they do it quickly and instinctively. We can slow down and unpick that speedy approach, and get students to walk through the thinking of the person that created the model example. If they can 'think aloud' through the requisite steps toward excellence, we can be confident that they can go on to reproduce excellence in their own learning. They can explain their thinking behind their own choices, or work on trying to sequence the thinking of somebody else's work.

- **Peer tutoring.** Given structured support and the requisite prior knowledge, students can tutor one another through the learning process. With some judicious pairing of students (a great deal of existing peer tutoring is 'cross-age tutoring' – that is to say, older students teaching younger students) in your classroom, students can pose the questions outlined earlier in the chapter, such as 'Why did you start with that idea?' or 'Have you checked through to see that it makes sense?' or more simply, 'Have you forgotten to do X?' Doing this after some 'live feedback' from the teacher can prove particularly useful, as students can effectively mimic the teacher. Clear parameters of time, role, and the steps that students need to undertake through the tutoring process needs training and practice.

IN SHORT...

- Our lazy brains resist thinking hard about our own thinking, so it takes effort and self-control to do so.
- We need to help our students more consciously practice how to plan, monitor and evaluate their own learning. They will need support and strategies to undertake these metacognitive processes.
- We should see independent learning as a desirable end goal of schooling that requires a great deal of skilled training and modelling.
- Social modelling – such as the teacher exemplifying their thinking processes, to peers teaching one another – can help develop self-confident learners.
- Modelling excellence is essential for successful learning. When students see, hear and experience excellence, it can prove a transformative learning experience.

Notes

1 Claxton, G., quoted at the Futurelab conference, 'Beyond the exam: New directions in assessment', November 2003.

2 Kirschner, P.A., Sweller, J. and Clark, R.E. (2006), 'Why minimal guidance during instruction does not work: An analysis of the failure of constructivist, discovery, problem-based, experiential, and inquiry-based teaching', *Educational Psychologist*, 41 (2): 75–86.

3 Mills, K., Goddings, A. and Blakemore, S. (2014), 'Drama in the teenage brain', *Front Young Minds.* 2 (16). doi: 10.3389/frym.2014.00016.

4 McLeod, S.A. (2014), 'Bobo doll experiment'. [Online]. Available at: www.simplypsychology.org/bobo-doll.html (Accessed: 11 February 2015).

5 Lin-Siegler, X., Shaenfield, D. and Elder, A.D. (2015), 'Contrasting case instruction can improve self-assessment of writing', *Educational Technology Research and Development*, 1–21. doi: 10.1007/s11423-015-9390-9.

14 Memory for learning

Remember Rememb...

It is said that memory is the mother of all wisdom, but too often in education it is misjudged and derided as a near-robotic recall of facts.

Apparently, teachers with memory in mind are busy merely filling buckets and not lighting the fire of learning. We need to get it right and reclaim a focus on enhancing our students' faculty for memory as an essential part of confident teaching and learning.

Let's start with a question: what subject in our curriculum is most reliant upon our faculty for memory?

Martin Robinson, writer and ex-drama teacher, poses an answer that may not have been your first thought: drama.

He explains how memory is woven into each thought and act in drama lessons:

'Remembering lines, remembering how to say lines, remembering how to be and not to be, remembering when to breathe in and breathe out and hold your breath and when to laugh and cry and remembering how to laugh and how to cry... and how to invest in your emotion memory, your movement memory, and how to remember what everyone else says and does, how to remember how to act and react in a way that makes it look as though this is the first time this has ever occurred to you...'[1]

With this description we are reminded of the dynamic nature of memory and how it is an integral part of all of our thinking and feeling across the span of the curriculum.

As you read this chapter, you are utilising your memories of how to read and the English language, whilst drawing upon what you already know about human memory.

An active focus on memorisation – a useful tool for learning – is clearly only a minor part of the big picture of memory for learning.

We know that the human memory is not an easy thing to pin down for easy answers about teaching. There can prove a thin line between memory and imagination. Our all-too-human memory lacks the orderliness of a computer memory and it can prove maddeningly unreliable, but we can still find useful answers about how our students can learn better from the known science of the human memory.

I have spent the majority of my career as a teacher not really understanding the essential role of memory for learning. My misconceptions weren't the product of simple ignorance – they were formed by myths that permeate education, such as the mistaken notion that remembering mere titbits of knowledge is pointless in the electronic era of Google. Add to that the falsehoods that we use only 10 per cent of our brain, or that we are 'left brain' or 'right brain' learners.

There are legions of other memory myths. Have you heard the story of the so-called 'learning pyramid'? You know the one: you learn and remember only 10 per cent of what you read but a whopping 75 per cent of what you practice doing. Well, it's nonsense: what we remember is about so much more than just *how* you receive the information. I may listen to the radio during my car ride home from school, before then listening to a podcast in the comfort of my home: I hear them both, but what I remember will not prove equal.

There is a huge range of factors that impact upon how well we remember, beyond just how we receive information. How much we already know about the material to be remembered matters; how old the person is doing the remembering matters; how many times they have been exposed to the material matters. Knowing these factors can help us better influence the learning capacity of our students who are grappling to remember a curriculum bursting with knowledge and skills.

A little understanding can go a long way. Take the hippocampus, a seahorse-shaped structure within the brain. It plays an important function in forming new memories and it is like a gateway to our long-term memory. We know that stress damages the healthy functioning of the hippocampus. Children who lack confidence and who are stressed and anxious simply can't remember what they learn as well. Clearly, our function to remember then influences so much of what we do when we aim to create the conditions for successful learning.

We can learn interesting but informative anomalies about our memory in action. Most of us draw upon so many memories from a photograph, but what if taking photographs actually hampers our memory? A research study by Linda Henkel showed that undergraduates who took photographs of objects in a museum performed worse on an object recognition test the day after compared to those who simply observed the objects.[2]

What does this *photo-taking impairment effect* mean for teachers? Well, it may reveal a crucial factor for enhancing our students' memory: focus. It is once more back to hard thinking. Our students best remember what they think hardest about. Distraction and interference is an enemy of memory for learning. It may also tell us that in a world stuffed full of selfies we may miss out on some important stuff.

When confronted with weapons of mass distraction, focusing on hard thinking is no easy task. For our students, the importance of focus cannot be overstated.

Take the simple task of reading this chapter in the book. It is easy to drift in and out of focusing hard: our brains are lazy and constantly looking for an exit strategy from hard thinking. It proves no easier from a student's perspective. We need to guide them to focus better. Simply asking our students to summarise the chapter visually, or in a short written summary, makes them pay more attention and focus on what they have read.

It is too easy to take for granted what our students are learning and what they are likely to remember. I now realise just how essential it is for teachers to know how memory works and why it is inextricably linked to how we learn successfully. In each lesson we teach, a simple plan for what we want our students to focus upon, and how we will get them to do so, really matters.

So how do we fix our common and often collective memory lapses? Jettisoning erroneous brain myths will save us time, whilst developing our knowledge of the science of learning and the growing brain can help us better develop our confidence about what works in the classroom.

Memorable learning and the growing brain

As we learnt from how experts 'chunk' information (remember breaking down a phone number into parts?) to better organise and remember their knowledge in Chapter 4, we learn better when we break things down into more memorable chunks. Three is our magic number in the case of memory for learning, as there are three important 'stages of memory'.

Let's explore the three stages of memory.

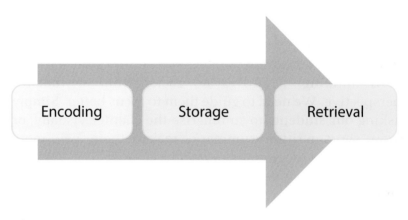

Figure 14.1

Encoding

When we receive information into our memory we must first encode it – that is to say, we change it into something we know and can manage effectively. We use visual (picture), acoustic (sound) and semantic (meaning) cues to help encode something in our memory.

Take the phone number 'chunking' example. We may quickly look at the number and break it down into digestible visual chunks, such as when we are looking to learn a spelling, for example: *fav – our – ite*. To help us encode it further we may sound it out to ourselves a few times (acoustic), before then associating it with our new favourite friend at the end of the phone line (semantic).

The more memory cues, like the visual cue above, the better encoded a memory becomes. Here, repetition and repeated exposure to cues and related information is essential. Practice is essential. The more students practice, the stronger they encode the given information.

Considering how and when we will repeat key information and how we will practice the required knowledge and skills in each lesson requires careful planning. If you want students to learn cellular structures in science, for example, you need to carefully plan how you will encode that knowledge best.

Storage

How and where we store our memories is crucial.

The simplest description of the process of storage is that we first receive information in our short-term memory. This has a very limited capacity of about seven items (between five and nine pieces of information at any one time).[3]

For example, if you are reading this chapter, you may be juggling with different pieces of information: you may be visualising a brain and a storage facility, whilst thinking of your best friend, alongside thinking of making a cup of coffee and maybe thinking of picking up your dry cleaning.

This constant juggle of information lasts for a few seconds. The important stuff – hopefully, you're thinking about the brain and storage – then transfers to your long-term memory. This is the crucial destination for teachers. If something is learnt and stored in our long-term memory then we are capable of retrieving it again. To remember this chapter may take a few repeated goes at reading chunks of it. You may make notes or deploy some well-placed Post-it® notes.

The better we chunk information, the more likely we are to store it in our long-term memory. When we chunk information down we then create a greater capacity for storage.

Try this little test. Here is a list of not-so-random words:

apple chair cherry pen orange whiteboard peas carrots paper broccoli

Now, give yourself thirty seconds and focus upon remembering the words. After that do something else for five or ten minutes. Tear yourself away from the book ('How could I possibly!' I hear you cry) and make yourself a drink, or grab yourself a snack.

Finally, once you have returned, test how many of the words from the list you can remember.

Crucially, how much we can store proves finite, but if we deploy clever tactics, like chunking and creating multiple cues, we can boost our storage capacity.

How did you go about the task? Did you chunk the words into categories: fruit, vegetables and classroom materials? Did you visualise the objects, or verbally rehearse the list? Or did you deploy a clever combination of these strategies?

Activating these multiple strategies can of course improve the memory of our students. When we give them verbal explanations (auditory cues) we can use images (visual cues) and we can hook into their prior knowledge and use striking metaphors (semantic cues).

Psychologists have labelled this capacity to deal with information as our 'working memory'. Imagine a postal worker dealing with letters and deliveries coming into the post depot. They organise and arrange the different delivery types and categorise them into postal codes. We, and our students, are doing the same each lesson. Each topic is a postal code, with many houses within its span.

After the crucial organising job at the depot – the working memory – then deliveries can happen.

Working memory, our capacity to juggle pieces of information in our short-term memory at any one time, is a crucial cognitive skill for our students. Their working memory skill is shown to correlate with ability in reading and maths for five and six year olds and for eleven and twelve year olds. It is even argued that it is a better predictor of future academic success than IQ.[4]

How important it is in relation to general intelligence is subject to debate, but our awareness of the limits and the potential of working memory is no doubt useful and valuable for planning how to best teach. Just consider: how does the limited nature of our students' short-term memory (seven different items in a given lesson) impact upon your lesson planning?

Of course, adults have a more developed working memory than children, so this can impact how and what we teach to students of different ages. As we know instinctively, we can teach more challenging knowledge with greater frequency to older children, but principles of practice and repetition hold fast for us all.

We must also be aware to not overload our students with too much information – particularly new and unfamiliar knowledge – at any one time. They simply won't be able to manage and they may not have the expert strategies of chunking or multiple cueing to hand that we take for granted as seasoned learners.

Retrieval

Our students need to be able to grab their memories out of storage in long-term memory at will. This skill is crucial, but it isn't as straightforward as we would hope.

We all have experienced countless hours in school studying a subject that we can remember precious little about. Some memories fade and others disappear, seemingly altogether, only to reappear with a sensory trigger. Eating a biscuit can spark the memory recall from the deepest recesses of your long-term memory.

Strengthening the retrieval capacity of our students is essential. The more recent an event or information is to us, like the snack we have just devoured, the higher its retrieval strength, but unless it was a truly important snack then you will soon forget it. Compare that to a personal memory that has a great deal of meaning to you – like the birth of a child, a wedding day, or a university graduation. Because it is important to us, we have thought about it a great deal and that has increased the retrieval strength of this memory.

What are the implications for the classroom?

Well, repeated practice can help strengthen information retrieval. Couple repeated practice with making the memory interesting and generating strong emotional associations, and we will increase the likelihood of remembering. This can come from the power of a great teacher-student relationship, but it can be created with a conscious attempt to make the learning emotionally meaningful.

A field trip, by the simple means of it being a unique and collaborative experience, can be more memorable than a classroom explanation. Of course, we can't engineer a school trip for every act of learning, but engineering significant learning experiences like this can prove motivating and deeply memorable.

Take a topic that is coming up for one of your classes. How can you strategically approach those three steps of encoding, storing and retrieving the material so that the topic is as memorable as possible? What cues will you generate? How will you artfully repeat explanations and acts of practice with memorable effect? How will you know the right information has been transferred to long-term memory?

There are many strategies related in this section on 'Confident Pedagogy' that explicitly help students improve their memory. Let's recap just some of them:

- **Hook in new knowledge to the existing knowledge of our students.** E. D. Hirsch described deep prior knowledge as 'mental Velcro'. Simply put, we stick new knowledge to what we already know. Therefore, having a vast existing store of knowledge proves pretty important. Planning our schemes of learning to strategically accumulate this wealth of powerful knowledge is crucial.
- **Get students to ask lots of challenging questions.** The more students probe and question information, the deeper they process it in their long-term memory.
- **Think-pair-share.** Get students thinking and discussing new knowledge and skills. Again, the more we get our students thinking and talking and elaborating upon the subject, the stronger the encoding of the memory.
- **Build a 'memory palace'.** This ancient strategy draws upon the memorable cues of visual imagery and stories to devise an elaborate edifice of memorable knowledge.
- **Tell memorable stories; use striking visual metaphors and analogies.** I don't need to tell you a story to reiterate this notion, I hope!
- **Create visual imagery to cue information.** Graphic organisers, like Venn diagrams or concept maps, all work on the same principle of organising, connecting and making visible patterns of meaning to make memories. Be it a 'topic triptych', flashcards, model examples, question walls, checklists, 'triplicate note-making' or a '"How to" guide', we draw upon knowledge

that is clearly structured and most often visibly memorable.

'Just don't call it a test'

Let's begin with a multiple-choice question. Which of the following best describes your definition of the term 'test' when applied to education?

a) An out-of-date token of an exam-factory school model that is damaging our students' learning
b) A blunt tool that is used to clobber teachers at every available opportunity
c) A vital tool for education
d) You are too surprised by option c) to give an intelligent response.

We have a problem. We have very little confidence in the notion of 'testing' being in any way positive in our schools.

Get teachers (or students, or parents for that matter) to answer this multiple-choice question and the answers are likely to be variations on options a) and b). This is because it is seemingly impossible to distinguish the idea of testing from the deep-seated prejudices we have about our high-stakes exam regime. Do this we must, because testing doesn't just measure our students; more importantly, it is an effective tool for improving learning.

The benefits of learning through testing are many, even if they seem counter-intuitive at first. For example, rather than leave a test until the end of a topic or scheme of learning, research suggests that we should start with one. It also suggests that we should test more, using regular low-stakes assessments, such as quizzes or short questions, to harness the power of memory for learning.

This is nothing new. The positive impact that taking a test has on students' ability to retain information is long-standing. Back in 1917, psychologist Arthur I. Gates explained the beneficial impact of testing, or 'recitation' as it was termed, on learning.[5] More recently, a range of professors busy uncovering the science of memory and learning have supported the notion that tests (low stakes, formative tests that don't seek to judge the student or the teacher) can have a strong positive impact on our students, strengthening their memory for what they have learnt.[6]

First, we need to start with a little rebranding. There is a stark difference between high-stakes exams and low-stakes testing for learning. Testing in this sense could involve students simply being quizzed on taught topics (a 'quiz' doesn't sound as daunting as a test).

Cognitive psychologists have grasped the importance of relabeling 'testing', so they labelled it 'retrieval practice' instead. They are onto something – 'retrieval practice' doesn't sound half as intimidating as testing.

Simply getting students to remember what they know and map it out on a piece of paper at the start of a lesson is a 'test' of a sort. It proves trickier than students re-reading their notes and copying them out, but that *deliberate difficulty* (a term coined by cognitive psychologist Robert Bjork) of not having their notes, makes it harder to retrieve the information in the first instance, but when retrieved, the very same information is more strongly encoded in long-term memory.

We have all experienced the phenomenon. Trying to revise without any notes is much harder than having a book to hand; yet, ultimately, we remember more from working without the support tools to rely on. This should help us consider some of our teaching strategies with their degree of 'difficulty' in mind.

If we can support our students to self-regulate their studying and be resilient in the face of difficulty, they may find that their memory is stronger for it.

We should be wary in the knowledge that our students, quite understandably, will reject the notion of embracing added difficulty. Revising from notes and avoiding self-testing will always *feel* better and that counts for a great deal.

We have a job to do in convincing our students, and perhaps even ourselves, that more low-stakes testing is hugely valuable.

The timing of tests is important, too. As mentioned earlier, taking a test before beginning a topic can be very effective. Evidence has shown that even when students bombed on a test before studying the topic, they still learned more effectively in the long term.[7] This may seem intuitive, and we can easily be tempted to avoid such an experience of failure for our students; however, as we know, failure can be an essential ingredient for long-term success.

There is the danger that flunking a test may hit the confidence of a student, but if they trust our methods (we can and should explain our approach to our students) they can learn from their failures and gain in confidence and competence.

There are, of course, hurdles to overcome in this approach. The mere mention of testing will trigger fear and loathing in many teachers. The very notion of students struggling on a pre-test seems unacceptable. But there are benefits to 'learning ugly' and we must share and communicate these better.

Repeat, repeat, repeat

We all possess the common sense notion that if we repeat something enough, then we will better learn and remember it. We know that when it comes to memory for learning that repeated exposure to material could strengthen the memory, encoding it more strongly.

So, is repetition the answer to forgetting?

Hermann Ebbinghaus, a German psychologist over a century ago, used himself as a guinea pig to test forgetting over time. He showed that memories have a half-life and that we need to revisit materials to encode them in our long-term memory – so far so obvious. More usefully, he also explored the notion of 'overlearning': defining it as the number of repetitions of material after it can then be recalled one hundred per cent.

For example, I learnt Spanish at school (badly, alas). At an early stage I learnt to count to twenty in Spanish – reaching a perfect score on a test. Any rehearsal of the number sequence after that initial perfect test would be considered overlearning.

Overlearning then represents the common 'use it or lose it' strategy of repeating and revising materials that is enacted in classrooms everywhere. Sadly, I have lost nearly my entire fledgling Spanish.

A common example of overlearning is how students revise for an exam. Given a test on the causes of the First World War in history, students may re-read their notes over and over (re-reading is the most common revision strategy undertaken by the majority of students)[8] until they can remember the material with confidence. The problem here is that we can quickly become too confident once we become very familiar with the material. Students can then stop their revision too early – overconfident of their readiness – developing a powerful illusion of competence.[9]

Strategies like re-reading, or simply highlighting notes, prove to be an example of shallow repetition and not deep learning. When people criticise rote learning they are right in that repetition alone is not enough. How well our students remember the material we teach is not simply down to how frequently they revise it or practice it, but what strategies they deploy in so doing.

We come back to the 'testing effect'. If we deploy formative tests then we can be more confident in their success. Strategies like using flashcards, self-quizzing, undertaking past exams, reconstructing their notes into striking visual designs and asking, and answering lots of questions on a given topic, will likely work given some well-judged repeated practice.[10]

What then is well-judged repetition? Well, cognitive scientists can help us here too. In the study of effective learning, they have found the counter-intuitive answer to a better memory for learning: forgetting.

The counter-intuitive part is that the bigger the gap – or the 'spacing effect' – between information being repeated actually strengthens our capacity to remember and retrieve that information in future.

Now, for most of us teachers we teach in topics or blocks. In chemistry, for example, you may teach a unit on atoms and elements en masse, then move on to chemical reactions and oxidation. Students learn a topic, sometimes never fully revisiting that knowledge, and we assume it is learnt. This 'massed practice', studying a topic all at once, feels fluent and natural, but the problem is it is too easy and too fluent. Like my GCSE Spanish, it can be quickly forgotten. We can all too easily become overconfident in what we have learnt. 'Massed practice' then can prove another example of repeated learning that is too shallow.

Instead, we can go about mixing different topics up – described as the process of 'interleaving' – thereby placing increasingly bigger gaps in between studying a topic and repeating the study of the topic. We force the brain to do a harder job remembering, but this difficulty is what actually makes the knowledge stick.[11]

For example, in mathematics you would typically see geometry and algebra taught separately, but with an interleaved approach you could teach algebraic equations, then geometric symmetry, before then returning to algebraic equations. Though seemingly disorganised, and perhaps trickier to plan, this method naturally spaces out the material, inducing some constructive forgetting. This forgetting, as we know, paradoxically, would likely strengthen our students' memory of the mathematical content.

Typical 'massed practice', teaching topics in blocks, looks like this in a lesson sequence:

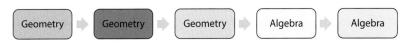

Figure 14.2

By 'interleaving', you mix up the topics, making it trickier in the first instance, but more memorable in the long term because students have had to think a little harder. In a lesson sequence it looks like this:

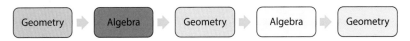

Figure 14.3

We can make this eminently practical by using quizzes and other low-stakes testing approaches to do the job of interleaving for us. If we spend a week studying geometry, we can then quiz students at the end of the week on algebraic equations. We can move onto the study of algebraic equations, but start some lessons with a quick reminder and quiz on geometric problems.

Both *spacing* and *interleaving* can both be described as 'desirable difficulties' and they nicely complement one another. Students are forced to think harder and focus more, but in this state students better remember what they learn. This is what we can then describe as artful repetition.

These approaches, like some testing approaches, may even hamper self-confidence in the short term, but we gain greater competence and authentic confidence in the long term. Students may not make speedy progress in the short term, but instead they will better remember by undertaking difficult and slower, but, ultimately, deeper learning.

Take a moment to consider how this may work in a practical sense. Over the course of a week, or more long term over a span of months, how might it look with one of your classes?

The evidence from the science of learning, alongside a greater understanding of the learning brain, gives us much to ponder about the strategies we deploy in the classroom and how we structure our curriculum most effectively. By knowing and understanding the scientific basis of how our students remember, we can fuel ourselves with greater confidence in our SPK that we exercise in the classroom.

Useful strategies to deploy the 'testing effect' to enhance our students' memory:

- **Mnemonics.** This age-old strategy works by helping students cue their memory with more complex information. A vast swath of knowledge about a period in history can be reduced to a single mnemonic, helping 'chunk' down information for students. For example, the royal families of England – Norman, Angevin, Plantagenet, Lancaster, York, Tudor, Stuart, Hanover and Windsor – becomes the mnemonic: *Neighbours actually persuaded lovely Yvonne to shut her window.*
- **Flashcards.** A long-standing staple of revision sessions the world over, flashcards draw upon many of the facets that support better memory encoding. First, they get students to summarise and reconstruct material into a

condensed form, before then providing the opportunity for regular self-testing/quizzing. They are easy and highly effective mini-tests.

- **Take the pre-test.** As already stated, a pre-test can be extremely effective; however, you have to ensure that it's used positively. Follow up the test by identifying the gaps in students' understanding, giving them precise feedback on their misconceptions and using this assessment to plan meaningful future study. You can also fix any potential damage to pupils' self-confidence by highlighting how far they've moved on from the pre-test as you progress through a topic.

- **Forgetting fortnight.** This strategy is borrowed from my PE teaching colleague, Nigel Currie. He found that his A-level PE students learnt the difficult topics in the short term, but their memory waned in the long term. One such topic, year upon year, had foxed his students: *arterio-venous oxygen difference (a-vo2 diff.).* The solution: *spacing* and *interleaving* practise using his 'forgetting fortnight' method. After the initial teaching of this tricky topic, Nigel gave his students a short test. He then gave them a fortnight to forget. After a couple of repeat tests, students showed that they had better encoded the tricky knowledge of a-vo2 diff.

- **The main thing...weekly review.** Akin to 'forgetting fortnight', conducting a weekly review of learning utilises the power of spacing for memory retention. Now, most teachers feel the pressures of getting through the content of the curriculum, but if it isn't in the long-term memory of our students then we only create problems later on. A quick weekly review can take little time, but it can have a big impact.

IN SHORT...

- Memory is much more than merely rote learning; it is the dynamic stuff of *all* learning.
- We should aim to strengthen the encoding of memories, using images and sounds, alongside any other stimulus that helps students strengthen their memories of what is being taught.
- The 'testing effect', or 'retrieval practice', doesn't signal the death of modern education – instead, it is an essential approach, when wedded to other strategies, which can make your teaching truly memorable.
- Students invariably revise badly, and with overconfidence, so we need to teach them to revise with memory in mind.
- The principles of cognitive science and memory for learning, such as spacing, chunking, interleaving and more, should guide our lesson planning and aid our curriculum design.

Notes

1   Robinson, M. (2015), 'Memory'. [Online]. Available at: https://martinrobborobinson.wordpress.com/2015/05/05/memory/ (Accessed: 17 August, 2015).
2   Henkel, L.A. (2014), 'Point-and-shoot memories: The influence of taking photos on memory for a museum tour', *Psychological Science*, 25: 396–402.
3   Miller, G. (1956), 'The magical number seven, plus or minus two: Some limits on our capacity for processing information', *The Psychological Review*, 63: 81–97.
4   Alloway, T.P. and Alloway, R.G. (2010), 'Investigating the predictive roles of working memory and IQ in academic attainment', *Journal of Experimental Child Psychology*, 106: 20–29.

5   Gates, A.I. (1917), 'Recitation as a factor in memorizing'. University of California Libraries. Available at: https://archive.org/details/recitationasafaoogategoog (Accessed: 5 January 2015).

6   Pashler, H., Bain, P., Bottge, B., Graesser, A., Koedinger, K., McDaniel, M. and Metcalfe, J. (2007), 'Organizing instruction and study to improve student learning', (NCER 2007–2004). Washington, DC: National Center for Education Research, Institute of Education Sciences, U.S. Department of Education [Online]. Available at: http://ncer.ed.gov (Accessed: 3 June 2014).

7   Richland, L.E., Kornell, N. and Kao, L.S. (2009), 'The pretesting effect: Do unsuccessful retrieval attempts enhance learning?', *Journal of Experimental Psychology: Applied*, 15 (3): 243–257.

8   Karpicke, J.D., Butler, A.C. and Roediger III, H.L. (2009), 'Metacognitive strategies in student learning: Do students practise retrieval when they study on their own?', *Memory*, 17 (4): 471–479.

9   Karpicke, J.D., Butler, A.C. and Roediger III, H.L. (2009), 'Metacognitive strategies in student learning: Do students practise retrieval when they study on their own?', *Memory*, 17 (4): 471–479.

10 Dunlovsky, J. et al. (2013), 'Improving students' learning with effective learning techniques: Promising directions from cognitive and educational psychology', *Psychological Science in the Public Interest* 14 (1): 4–58.

11 Birnbaum, M.S., Kornell, N., Bjork, E.L. and Bjork, R.A. (2012), 'Why interleaving enhances inductive learning: The roles of discrimination and retrieval' [Online]. Available at: http://bjorklab.psych.ucla.edu/pubs/Birnbaum_Kornell_EBjork_RBjork_inpress.pdf (Accessed: 10 August 2014).

Section 4
Confident learners

15 Bridging the confidence gap

Like any self-respecting English teacher, I like to tell stories to my students. One such story is the embodiment of a flourishing, confident learner. It is the story of a little girl from North Carolina, USA, and it is a real-life story that shines a light on the amazing capacity of young people to learn.

It is the story of Cameron Mott – the girl with half a brain.

Cameron's young childhood was cruelly beset with crippling seizures that attacked her brain. The video of her online having one of these debilitating fits is harrowing. At only three years old, her rare condition – Rasmussen's syndrome – quickly destroyed her fledgling brain with each seizure. The frankly terrifying solution was for surgeons to remove half of little Cameron's brain. After the radical surgery Cameron, as expected, was paralysed in the left side of her body (the side of her brain controlled by the removed right side of her brain).

Then the awe-inducing plasticity of the young girl's paediatric brain took over. Within a month Cameron was walking again. Within a short span of years, Cameron was a healthy girl living a life of miraculous normality. Free of her debilitating seizures, young Cameron now dreams of becoming a ballerina.

The plasticity of the human brain – with our related capacity to learn – is tremendously malleable. Undoubtedly, we are all born with a unique genetic heritage, but our growth, how we are nurtured and taught, can change the path of our lives. If our students understand this and believe in their own capacity to grow and flourish then they can better gain the confidence to take on any challenge. The courage of Cameron Mott is an inspirational story that can nourish such a belief.

As teachers, we are in control of a legion of factors that can grow or diminish the potential of our students to become confident and successful learners. We are gifted with students like Cameron whose brain is malleable, hungry to learn, and full of curiosity.

The turmoil of the teen brain

Beyond the rare stories like the one I have just described, you would be forgiven for thinking that each generation of children is worse than the last. The media is quick to characterise teens as 'yobs', 'thugs' and worse. We hear repeated calls that technology and the Internet are damaging their brains and eroding their morals. Only there isn't any dumbing down of our children. In fact, scientists have identified the *Flynn Effect*: a steady rise in IQ from the 1930s to the present day.

Our modern world, it would appear, suffers from *ephebiphobia*: a fear of young people.

This is nothing new. In the fourth century BC, Plato, when he wasn't busy philosophising about caves, complained about teenagers disrespecting their elders and lamenting their 'decaying morals' and wild notions. Then and now, we shouldn't believe the hype. Yes, every teacher has felt some mildly ephebiphobic tendencies every once in a while, but we also know not to believe the scare stories.

The growing brain is undoubtedly beset by emotional upheaval. The limbic system – the complex region of the brain that governs emotion, instinct and mood – actually rewards risky behaviour during the teenage years. Not only that, the pre-frontal cortex, that manages such impulses, is undergoing radical changes too. It is our job, *in loco parentis*, to help our students negotiate their way through this emotional maze and out of the other side into adulthood.

'Yobs' and 'thugs' they are not, but adolescent children in particular are prone to taking risks and losing their self-control, seeing them test our boundaries and sometimes our patience.

We know that these emotional changes instigated in the brain make students acutely sensitive to their social identity and how they relate to others. Their sense of belonging to their social groups can even supplant their parental relationship for a time.

Teachers – well, we face some of their emotional ire in this struggle for selfhood. We see peer pressure for both good and ill, with our job being to harness the power of peer role models for the better.

We know that boys in particular can struggle to control their emotions and their behaviour when faced with a

Bridging the confidence gap

disorganised setting,[1] whereas girls do a better job of managing their own behaviour. With this in mind, in mixed gender schools, we can better consider our student groupings and more sensitively arrange and manage our classroom space.

How our students respond to their peers is no doubt influenced by factors like gender. There is a 'stereotype threat' at work: both boys and girls can feel at risk socially, as standing out as different from their peers threatens them with being isolated and losing their precious sense of belonging. Incidents like bullying can be strong reactions to these tumultuous emotions.

Changes in their school life can prove traumatic and damage the fragile confidence of our students. The transition from primary school to secondary school can prove a seismic shift for many students. Secondary schools can make our students feel anonymous compared to their much smaller primary counterparts. Students can therefore feel lost, and when faced with the more plentiful work and the more challenging academic demands at secondary school, their self-confidence can crumble.

There can prove a subtle *'big fish, little pond effect'*. Students who had gone about comparing themselves favourably with their peers in their smaller primary setting are then faced with a range of new subjects and little more to gauge their skill other than comparing themselves once more with their peers. With many more fish in this particular pond, and a quick-fire sensitivity to feelings of inferiority and social difference, it can prove a toxic combination.

We once more return to the threat of overconfidence.

Students who had thrived at primary school using a particular set of tools then become reliant upon them and unwilling to change their approach.[2] When they fail, their self-confidence can be crippled and they can become quickly turned off from learning.

266

Ironically, committing effort to a task can prove damaging to their sense of belonging. When their friend is comfortably tackling a mathematics task, for example, it can prove 'natural' to our students to give up and say it is too hard, as they simply aren't good enough by way of comparison.

We see it every day in our classrooms: students' attitudes and beliefs merge to fit in with their group and the emotional climate of such groups can change how they approach their learning and how they respond to us.

Disaffected groups can quickly harden and vice versa for those who are flourishing academically. We can perpetuate such a divide when we group students by their seeming ability (too often, it is factors like behaviour and not academic ability that really determine class groupings). Before long, students identify themselves in relation to their group, either for or against the teacher.

The reality of confidence being linked to our social ties means that we need to consciously foster confidence with groups of students in our classrooms and schools.

Organisations like The Sutton Trust exist to support students who don't have strong social ties to support them and who are therefore prone to having little confidence that they fit in academically. Dr. Lee Elliot Major, Chief Executive of The Sutton Trust, recognises the crucial role of the classroom teacher: 'One of the most inspiring things truly great teachers and schools do is instil in children the "have-a-go" confidence that their more privileged peers naturally pick up from their supportive middle class homes.'

Major also recognises that support for students must also extend beyond the classroom: 'The Sutton Trust's work to improve access for state school pupils into leading universities at its core is really about challenging the "not for the likes of me" or "I'm not good enough" attitudes that still prevail among swathes of children in our society. We

267

know these children have the talents to flourish in higher education; they just need that inner confidence to fulfil their academic potential.'

We know 'inner-confidence' can prove tricky to define, but the tools of the body and mind that are explored in this book, to be utilised by teachers, can prove equally useful for our students.

It is crucial that we don't make the mistake of seeking to boost our students' social confidence without focusing upon their academic competence. Major makes the point: 'While it is right that we focus on academic achievement of disadvantaged pupils in schools to enhance their life prospects, we also know that children's attitudes to learning and their social skills more broadly are just as key to improving social mobility. Ideally, you want to do both.'

Major also notes that there are important 'transition points in children's lives when they are most at risk'. Moving schools, going from primary to secondary school, or leaving school to go to university, are times that crucially require the nurturing support of teachers and more.

The reality of confidence and self-belief being tied to the social groups around us, which we feel we belong to, never really goes away.

It becomes our essential task as teachers to give our students a strong sense of belonging in our classroom. Students feel it instinctively. The best teachers cultivate this sense of belonging with a deep authenticity and it is realised in their words and their every action.

It becomes a matter of collective confidence. Students see their peers persevering through failure and committing effort and it becomes normal, simply part of what the group does.

Small psychological nudges can help. Rather than saying that ten students have failed to complete their homework, thereby normalising this behaviour, we can deftly turn this on its head. By telling students how the vast majority of the group committed a huge effort to their homework, you can subtly make the small number who didn't do the homework feel apart from the typical group norms. Their pride pricked, they can quickly be brought back into the fold.

Some of our students will go a long way to protect their pride and to fit in with their peers. Being perceived as lazy is seen as normal for many teens (indeed, for some it can prove a badge of honour), whereas being seen as unintelligent is decidedly more negative. You can therefore have students, in an act of self-preservation, go about handicapping themselves: failing to work hard and getting into trouble.

Identifying this type of behaviour takes expertise and often a collective approach from every teacher in the school. A whole school culture can break down some of the hardened barriers that many of our teenagers build to insulate their fragile sense of identity. Hard thinking becomes 'natural', risk-taking is made safe, and confidence becomes positively tied to effort and achievement.

We can ask ourselves: what type of classroom culture are we going to foster? What habits and behavioural norms are we going to establish in our classroom and how are we going to go about it?

We needn't create a powder-puff culture of fake emotionalism and faint praise, but we do need to help our students feel safe and full of hope that they could do anything with their efforts and our support.

The power of expectation

Mr Laing was my year 8 maths teacher. He was a rare breed indeed. He helped me and my fellow pimple-clad peers find mathematics interesting. Intermittently, he would betray a deep excitement about a mathematics problem, or reveal that he had woken up in the middle of the night with an answer to some mathematics concept. We were incredulous. Being excited by mathematics was anathema.

Soon enough though, incredulity became intrigue. Over time, he made us think that such interest might even be possible for us too. I had never felt anything about mathematics before, but for a short time I did and it mattered.

Mr Laing had once been like us, he had told us. He told us stories about how he didn't like maths at school and how he had found it too difficult. He spoke about how he had persevered and something had inexplicably clicked in time. Though still difficult, it had become gradually easier. Without realising it then, he was proving the ideal role model for us to help us develop our confidence that we too could think like a mathematician and succeed. Albert Bandura would approve.

Over the course of a year or two, with the implicit language of high expectations and an unremitting belief in our capacity to be better at mathematics, many of us were beguiled. We became believers: in him, and most importantly, in ourselves.

When I later embarked upon becoming a teacher, I asked myself, what magic was this? What trickery could I imitate? As a teacher, now, I wrack my brains to remember the detail of what he did and what he said. I can't quite remember, I can only recall the lingering feeling he had created.

Sadly, and too soon, with different teachers, my instinctive aversion to mathematics returned. A lifetime of impressions from my family that we were 'natural' born readers and artistic types – *naturally* hopeless at mathematics – reasserted itself grimly. My own expectation of success in maths was diminished and my confidence dimmed.

Later on, with a better understanding of psychology and teaching, Mr Laing's magic became something less mysterious. The phenomenon of the *Pygmalion effect* goes some way to explaining the impact of Mr Laing on my motivation and my achievement in mathematics. This concept, that high expectations can foster improved performance, has been explored since the 1960s to the present day.

The power of the teacher as role model is something most of us experienced at school. Many teachers will readily account for a teacher who inspired them at school. It is a common truth that fuels teacher recruitment the world over. We must therefore be acutely aware of the expectations we convey and the mindset we model for our students in our every interaction and our every utterance.

Whether I thought I could learn maths or not, I was right. Sadly, when Mr Laing left my school my love of mathematics left with him. My confidence and competence wasn't yet deep rooted enough and so my effort drifted once more.

There is the flipside to the confidence-fuelling impact of the *Pygmalion effect*. Mr Laing, in a bleak parallel world of low expectations for friends and myself, could have exercised what is known as the *Golem effect*.

The Golem, a monster created by Rabbi Loew in Prague, in Hasidic mythology, was a creature made of clay, used as a tool for the Rabbi. Alas, one Sabbath, the Rabbi forgets to shut down his monster and, left to its own devices, the Golem is tragically destructive, before then being destroyed.

This mythic tale reveals that dark side of expectancy and confidence. If we expect students to fail then they may prove more likely to do so. Even a near-hidden indication of low expectations can have damaging effects on the achievement of our students. We may not do it with conscious intent, but when we group our students and let some students take a back seat, or we make the work easier when we face some resistance, we send out a message about our confidence in each student, or the lack thereof.

It is only natural to dismiss that we ourselves could be guilty of low expectations, but we can be confronted with some uncomfortable truths.

We do, quite instinctively, stereotype our students. Most often it is to make valuable shortcuts so that we may teach them better, but there can also be some negative judgements too. Evidence has unveiled that subtly negative stereotypes can be formed, based on the gender of children, or their family background and their social class.[3] Also, when teachers see students grouped in classes by ability that too can bias them against that student compared to another in a notional higher ability group.[4]

Our expectation can too easily become a lived reality.

One of the redeeming features of being a teacher is the endless annual renewal. Like flowers emerging in spring, our new classes begin *afresh, afresh, afresh,* and our expectancy can be renewed too. Each school year, each class, each relationship is a new start, with many students maturing and changing for the better. With each new start we can better align our expectations to be pitched higher than our students dare to believe.

With teachers like Mr Laing, who patently loved teaching mathematics, believing in the limitless potential of my friends and I, anything felt possible and we flourished. That memory has never left me and it informs how I try to teach.

We know that no one teacher teaches in splendid isolation. It takes a school, parents, peers and more, but each individual teacher can make a crucial difference.

A matter of mindset

We know that our expectations and our attitude towards our students matter a good deal, but those aren't the sole influence on our students' belief in their ability and their capacity to succeed in school. There is also the complex matter of the influence of their peers and the central role of parents or their caregivers.

Happily, I was brought up by my family to believe that you got your just rewards for working hard. It is a belief that has stayed with me and nourished me throughout my life.

Well, with an important qualification. You see, in my family we weren't very good at mathematics. In fact, nor were we *naturally* any good at the sciences. Instead, we were *naturally* good at subjects like English, history and art.

I think you can start to see the problem. Over time I worked harder at those subjects I could *do*, whilst sidelining the stuff I *naturally* wasn't any good at. Ultimately, after years of making a million small decisions about what I could or couldn't learn, my school qualifications became a self-fulfilling prophecy.

In truth, though we valued hard work, we didn't have much of a *growth mindset* in my family – at least when it came to mathematics and science. In the interim, I have learnt much about the plastic capacity of the brain to learn. The 'growth mindset' and 'fixed mindset' dichotomy, propounded by Carol Dweck, struck home with me as soon as I read her popular book, *Mindset: The Secret of Success*. She gave a language to my lived experience.

As shown in Chapter 12, the binary opposition of a *fixed* and a *growth* mindset is a simple but useful way to consider how our students' attitude can affect their capacity to learn. The messages are familiar. According to Dweck, a fixed-mindset student believes that intelligence is innate and fixed. With this state of affairs, any failure represents a personal failing and committing effort reflects a lack of 'natural' ability. Such an attitude can of course lead to an inability to persevere through difficulty and failure, alongside fostering a brittle self-confidence.

As explored in the section on feedback in Chapter 12, Dweck encourages teachers to help students develop a growth mindset by praising effort during the process of learning and not the person. Praise, and the nuances of language deployed by the teacher, matters. Simple words like 'yet' take on new meaning. 'I can't do mathematics' becomes 'I can't do mathematics *yet*'.

The notion of a growth mindset, with all the attendant research evidence, promises useful and useable strategies for teachers and a dose of good sense. We can change our language to ensure that we affect the confidence of our students in a positive fashion. Our written feedback can also be adapted to garner the most productive response from our students.

The concept of growth and fixed mindsets has quickly gained traction in schools. The message is so brilliantly simple and hopeful, and yet this simplicity could prove its greatest flaw.

A cluster of glossy and inspirational YouTube videos and motivational assemblies won't likely change anything for our students' self-confidence. Once more, we are threatened by instigating a superficial confidence that doesn't rightly address our students' competence first.

We can herald our students' efforts and we can eschew praising intelligence, but we must be keenly aware that the messages that we verbalise must be supported by our school systems and the strategies in our classrooms.

If we are to send the valuable message to students that they can improve with effort, but we then group them by ability in our classroom, or set them a target grade that is obviously below that of their peers, then we will likely drown out any positive impact of the subtle language we deploy.

What is a student to think when they sit through an assembly listening to a talk about the malleability of our intelligence, but then their best friend is selected for some special event because they are purportedly 'gifted and talented'? Is intelligence a 'gift', or is it something we enhance with effort? Our students can quickly grasp the jarring disconnect between language and action.

Well-meaning growth mindset sessions in schools may well prove popular for a short time, but they are likely to have a shallow effect on the minds of our students if we do not concurrently develop their subject knowledge and skills. Confidence stems from competence. Potentially laudable approaches, like promoting a growth mindset, will not prove a magic solution for teachers or for our students.[5]

We can give a psychological boost to our students' confidence, but we must wed this to giving them the right tools to best exercise their efforts. By exercising their competence, our students are given the tangible stuff that fuels a growth mindset.

The confidence gap

My confidence in mathematics ebbed and flowed with the subtle but unmistakable influence of my teacher. In a school packed with boys, a male role model certainly helped with my sense that I could become a confident and competent mathematician.

A significant amount of global research shows that there is a gender 'confidence gap' that we need to address in our schools. We know that role models and our students' self-concept matters. International research by PISA[6] has shown that even amongst students who perform at the same level, boys and girls can have radically different degrees of self-confidence in STEM (*science, technology, engineering and maths*) subjects in particular. This impact can be exacerbated with higher ability girls given their fragile sense of their success.

Bridging the confidence gap

Is it here, in the busy classroom full of students teeming with self-doubt and fragile confidence, when the female leaders of our future schools are created or lost?

On an annual basis, I have sat with highly competent girls who have flourished and achieved a great range of grades, but they obsess about a singular poor performance. Their fleet of top grades should fuel their confidence, but they are hampered by a singular 'failure'. Such emotional anxiety (specific mathematics anxiety is a real and troubling phenomenon) blocks the ability of our students to think hard and persevere in the face of problems and failures.

In STEM subjects, girls display modesty in the face of success and an obvious lack of confidence in the face of failure. Boys, in contrast, are more confident, even in the face of underperformance relative to their female peers. Though not likely a direct cause, it is a complex and multifaceted social issue; it is easy to see how women can prove so under-represented in STEM careers. It proves a vicious circle: a lack of female role models to inspire confidence for our female students sees the 'confidence gap' remain wide.

These confidence gaps don't just extend to a gender divide. Culturally, our students feel the intuitive impact of belonging in 'their group'. In a comparison of students from Japan and America, it showed that American students believed more in innate intelligence – you were born to study mathematics etc – whereas their Japanese counterparts believed that effort and studying hard was more important (twice as important as American students).[7] Not only that, their parents, unsurprisingly, believed the same. The cultural norm exhibited here can once more fuel a self-fulfilling prophecy for such students.

Confidence gaps are not exclusive to gender or cultural norms. Students from poorer backgrounds can have a confidence deficit with a similar reasoning: a lack of role models; an absence of confidence-fuelling social connections; the subtle lowering of expectations relative to the subjects they go on to study, and more. Indeed, when we consider the relative absence of females in taking STEM subjects, the picture is considerably worse when it comes to girls from low socio-economic backgrounds.[8]

With the teen brain so attuned to fitting in with their social group and to belonging, it is no surprise that confidence becomes a trait that is tied to others. As teachers, we cannot shift such potentially damaging stereotypes so deeply rooted in our culture, but we can create a micro-culture in our classroom. We can still defy beliefs that are tied to the limitations of innate ability, even whilst recognising that our genetic inheritance and the influence of those around us still matters.

It is clear that our confidence can be tied more narrowly to a subject discipline. Every subject has its heroines and heroes – stories each teacher can tell their students. In art, we can tell the story of Frieda Kahlo, who defied her lifelong health problems – stemming from a teenage car accident – to become an icon; or Vincent Van Gogh, who famously couldn't sell a canvas to save his ear, yet his genius has been etched eternally in the vaults of history.

Just as our novice students can imitate the brushstrokes of such artists, they can learn from the emotional challenges they faced. If these luminaries feel a little too far off, we can tell them stories of students from the ghosts of a year group from the past.

Memories of my past students bubble to the surface. One such student, Miles, had learned to dislike English with an unmitigated force. His irrational, but not untypical, hatred was rooted in his sense of failure that had developed over a period of years. He would give up on his writing at the earliest opportunity and so his English assessments became a depressing self-fulfilling prophecy.

Given even the smallest incitement, he could leave the lesson in anger. His confidence had been slowly but surely whittled away.

Miles would prove quiet and awkward from the start, resisting feedback on how to get better, but over time, with dogged persistence, we were able to develop a sense of mutual trust.

In private conversations, we talked through his anger and annoyance that would flare up intermittently, talking about how he could better manage his mood when he recognised the physical signs. Crucially, we focused in on some of his expert experiences in English: his sharply observed wit in his persuasive writing, or the sensual details of his descriptive writing. We continued to work on his weaknesses: his unthinking inaccuracy and his clumsy sentence structures. A sense of reciprocal vulnerability helped to broker our work, whereat we talked about the difficult emotions Miles felt when writing, just like I'd felt when learning mathematics.

Over a period of months, Miles grew his confidence as he improved far beyond basic competence.

It was a visible and physical process. He moved from his position near the back of the room, brooding and quiet, to near the front of the class, increasingly willing and interested. A reluctant teenage grunt softened into words and then fully fledged responses to questions. Almost imperceptibly, he stood a little taller, even committing himself to a temporary smile every once in a while.

Miles began to think and feel differently in his English class and it made all the difference.

The capacity to learn, change and grow, exhibited by Miles and Cameron Mott, is the stuff of a great education. With the leadership of a confident and expert teacher, students can learn and grow their self-belief that with commitment and effort they can be successful in school and beyond.

Great teaching is rooted in such beliefs: our belief in our students and their belief in themselves.

We return then to the roots of the word confidence: *confidere* – to have full trust. When Miles found it, things began to change for him. When we find trust and confidence in ourselves we too begin to thrive.

We need to work hard to develop our own professional confidence and competence so that we can then best help students like Miles to grow their confidence.

Students are relying upon us, putting their trust and confidence in us, to nurture them through the tricky emotional maelstrom of puberty and adolescence. Some prove unwilling, others are more receptive, but all are under our duty of care. Without self-indulgence or sentimentality, we can focus more on cultivating trusting relationships with our students. If we can prove reliable, open, honest, competent and confident,[9] then we prime our classrooms for great learning.

Yes, teaching and learning is about thinking hard and taking on academic challenges to secure a deeply rooted competence, but these are all founded upon an emotional relationship. At its most simple and at its most complex, in the open classroom and in the hidden pathways of the growing brain, teaching is an act of trust and love.

Remember, we should never doubt the power of a group of committed teachers to change the world given such trusting relationships, in a small way but no less truly, for each of our students and for one another.

IN SHORT...

- We need to better understand the complex terrain of how children learn if we are to have an authentic confidence in how we can best teach.
- We should avoid the temptation to create lessons in 'confidence building' and instead we should aim to develop our students' competence in thinking like an expert mathematician, artist, writer and more.
- Confidence in and of itself will not improve academic achievement, but academic achievement will likely grow alongside our students' confidence.
- Our attitude and beliefs, and those of our students, can powerfully influence the learning process.

Notes

1   Wachs, T.D., Gurkas, P. and Kontos, S. (2004), 'Predictors of preschool children's compliance behaviour in early childhood classroom settings', *Journal of Applied Developmental Psychology*, 25 (4): 439–457.
2   Schunk, D.H. and Pajares, F. (2004), 'Self-efficacy in education revisited: Empirical and applied evidence'. In D.M. McInerney and S. Van Etten (eds), *Big theories revisited*, pp. 115–138. Greenwich, CT: Information Age.
3   Campbell, T. (2015), 'Stereotyped at seven? Biases in teacher judgement of pupils' ability and attainment', *Journal of Social Policy*, 44 (3): 517–547.
4   Campbell, T. (2015), 'Stereotyped at seven? Biases in teacher judgement of pupils' ability and attainment', *Journal of Social Policy*, 44 (3): 517–547.
5   Yeager, D.S. and Walton, G.M. (2011), 'Social-psychological interventions in education: They're not magic', *Review of Educational Research*, 81 (2): 267–301.

6   OECD (2015), 'The ABC of gender equality in education: Aptitude, behaviour, confidence', PISA, OECD Publishing. [Online]. Available at: http://dx.doi.org/10.1787/978926422 9945-en (Accessed: 5 June 2015).

7   Stevenson, H.W., Chen, C. and Lee S., Y. (1993), 'Mathematics achievement of Chinese, Japanese, and American children: Ten years later', *Science*, 259: 53–58.

8   Codiroli, N. (2015), 'Inequalities in students' choice of STEM subjects: An exploration of intersectional relationships', UCL Institute of Education, CLS Working Paper 2015/16.

9   Hoy, W.K. and Tschannen-Moran, M. (2003), 'The conceptualization and measurement of faculty trust in schools'. In W.K. Hoy and C. Miskel (eds), *Studies in Leading and Organising Schools*, pp. 181–207. Greenwich, CT: Information Age.

Postscript

I have written this book at a challenging time for teachers. Tales of recruitment and retention crises, excessive workload and crippling stresses most often accompany the life of a teacher in the mass media.

Whilst I do not wish to ignore the very real problems that are felt by teachers, I want this book to help fuel the confidence of the legions of teachers who are determinedly making a real difference to the lives of their students, regardless of their school context.

I hold true to the belief that when we are the best version of ourselves, we can do great things as teachers.

It is said that achieving great things requires only two elements: a plan and not quite enough time. Teachers can easily lay claim to the latter, so this book is an attempt to provide a usable guide for the former.

Bibliography

Allison, S. and Tharby, A. (2015) *Every Lesson Counts: Six Principles to Support Great Teaching and Learning,* Camarthen: Crown House Publishing.

Baumeister, R.F. and Tierney, J. (2012) *Willpower: Rediscovering the Greatest Human Strength,* London: Penguin Books.

Bennett, T. (2012) *Teacher: Mastering the Art and Craft of Teaching,* London: Continuum Books.

Berger, R. (2003) *An Ethic of Excellence,* Portsmouth: Heinemann.

Brown, P.C., Roediger III, H.L. and McDaniel, M.A. (2014) *Make it Stick: The Science of Successful Learning,* London: The Belknap Press.

Bruning, R.H. et al. (1999) *Cognitive Psychology and Instruction, Fourth Edition,* Ohio: Pearson.

Burkeman, O. (2011) *HELP! How to Become Slightly Happier and Get a Bit More Done,* Edinburgh: Canon Gate Books.

Cain, S. (2012) *Quiet: The Power of Introverts in a World That Can't Stop Talking,* London: Penguin Books.

Chamorro-Premuzic, T. (2013) *Confidence: The Surprising Truth about How Much You Need and How to Get It,* London: Profile Books.

Dean, J. (2013) *Making Habits Breaking Habits,* London: Oneworld Publications.

Duhigg, C. (2012) *The Power of Habit,* New York: Random House.

Bibliography

Dweck, C. (2006) *Mindset: The New Psychology of Success*, New York: Ballantine Books.

Gawande, A. (2011) *The Checklist Manifesto: How to Get Things Right*, London: Profile Books Ltd.

Green, E. (2014) *Building A Better Teacher: How Teaching Works and How to Teach it to Everyone*, New York: W.W. Norton and Company.

Hattie, J. (2012) *Visible Learning for Teachers*, Oxon: Routledge.

Hattie, J. and Yates, G.C.R. (2014) *Visible Learning and the Science of How We Learn*, Oxon: Routledge.

Holmes, E. (2005) *Teacher Well-Being: Looking After Yourself and Your Career in the Classroom*, Oxon: Routledge.

James, W. (1899) *Talks To Teachers On Psychology And To Students On Some of Life's Ideals*, Public Domain Books.

Kahnemann, D. (2011) *Thinking Fast and Slow*, London: Penguin Books Ltd.

Kelsey, R. (2013) *What's Stopping You Being More Confident?*, Chichester: Capstone.

LaFrance, M. (2011) *Lip Service*, New York: W.W. Norton Company.

Lakoff, G. and Johnson, M. (1980) *Metaphors We Live By*, London: The University of Chicago Press.

Lemov, D. (2012) *Practice Perfect: 42 Rules for Getting Better at Getting Better*, San Francisco, CA: Jossey-Bass.

Lemov, D. (2010) *Teach like a Champion*, San Francisco, CA: John Wiley & Sons.

Mellanby, J. and Theobold, K. (2014) *Education and Learning: An Evidence-Based Approach*, Chichester: John Wiley & Sons.

Muijs, D. and Reynolds, D. (2011) *Effective Teaching: Evidence and Practice, Third Edition* (2011), London: Sage Publications.

Nuthall, G. (2007) *The Hidden Lives of Learners*, Wellington: NZCER Press.

Quigley, A. (2014) *Teach Now! Becoming A Great English Teacher*, Oxon: Routledge.

Richardson, P.W., Karabenick, S.A. and Watt, H.M.G. (2014) *Teacher Motivation: Theory and Practice*, Oxon: Routledge.

Rock, D. (2009) *Your Brain at Work*, New York: HarperCollins.

Sandberg, S. (2013) *Lean In: Women, Work and the Will to Lead*, London: WH Allen.

Stobart, G. (2014) *The Expert Learner: Challenging the Myth of Ability*, Berkshire: Open University Press.

Syed, M. (2011) *Bounce: The Myth of Talent and the Power of Practice*, London: Fourth Estate.

Tough, P. (2012) *How Children Succeed: Grit, Curiosity and the Hidden Power of Character*, London: Random House.

Turnbull, J. (2013) *9 Habits of Highly Effective Teachers: A Practical Guide to Personal Development*, London: Bloomsbury.

White, J. and Gardner, J. (2012) *The Classroom X Factor*, Oxon: Routledge.

Wiliam, D. (2011) *Embedded Formative Assessment*, Bloomington: Solution Tree Press.

Willingham, D.T. (2009) *Why Don't Students Like School?*, San Francisco: Jossey-Bass.

Index

Index

Taylor & Francis eBooks

Helping you to choose the right eBooks for your Library

Add Routledge titles to your library's digital collection today. Taylor and Francis ebooks contains over 50,000 titles in the Humanities, Social Sciences, Behavioural Sciences, Built Environment and Law.

Choose from a range of subject packages or create your own!

Benefits for you
» Free MARC records
» COUNTER-compliant usage statistics
» Flexible purchase and pricing options
» All titles DRM-free.

Benefits for your user
» Off-site, anytime access via Athens or referring URL
» Print or copy pages or chapters
» Full content search
» Bookmark, highlight and annotate text
» Access to thousands of pages of quality research at the click of a button.

REQUEST YOUR **FREE** INSTITUTIONAL TRIAL TODAY

Free Trials Available
We offer free trials to qualifying academic, corporate and government customers.

eCollections – Choose from over 30 subject eCollections, including:

Archaeology	Language Learning
Architecture	Law
Asian Studies	Literature
Business & Management	Media & Communication
Classical Studies	Middle East Studies
Construction	Music
Creative & Media Arts	Philosophy
Criminology & Criminal Justice	Planning
Economics	Politics
Education	Psychology & Mental Health
Energy	Religion
Engineering	Security
English Language & Linguistics	Social Work
Environment & Sustainability	Sociology
Geography	Sport
Health Studies	Theatre & Performance
History	Tourism, Hospitality & Events

For more information, pricing enquiries or to order a free trial, please contact your local sales team: www.tandfebooks.com/page/sales

Routledge
Taylor & Francis Group

The home of
Routledge books

www.tandfebooks.com